D1594944

THE HEART OF KARATE-DŌ

THE HEART OF KARATE-DO

Revised Edition

Shigeru Egami

KODANSHA INTERNATIONAL LTD.
Tokyo • New York • London

Previously published as "The Way of Karate"

Distributed in the United States by Kodansha America, Inc., 575 Lexington Avenue, New York, N.Y. 10022, and in the United Kingdom and continental Europe by Kodansha Europe Ltd., 95 Aldwych, London WC2B 4JF. Published by Kodansha International Ltd., 17-14 Otowa 1-chome, Bunkyo-ku, Tokyo 112-8652, and Kodansha America, Inc.

First original edition, 1975
First paperback edition, 1986
Revised edition, 2000
00 01 02 54321
ISBN4-7700-2477-0

Contents

Foreword 6
A Note from America 8
Preface 9
Introduction 11

  I PREPARATORY 21
        Warming-up Exercises 23
        Seiza 36

 II FUNDAMENTALS 39
        Stances 43
        Offensive Techniques 52
          Kicking 53
          Striking 64
        Blocking Techniques 79

III KATA 101

IV KUMITE 109

    Appendix I: Practice from a Sitting Position . . . 119
    Appendix II: Yin and Yang 122
    Index and Glossary 124
    Head Office and Branches of the Japan Karate-dō
      Shōtō-Kai 127
    Summary of Exercises and Techniques 129

Foreword

Many years have passed since the original publication of this book. This new edition has been put together in response to enthusiastic demands for its republication.

Master Gichin Funakoshi was the man who first introduced Okinawa's secret art of karate to mainland Japan, and he thereafter devoted himself to its dissemination. Master Funakoshi constantly taught that karate is not simply a fighting technique but rather an art that involves the cultivation of one's spiritual and mental energies, and indeed this was how he practiced karate.

Master Funakoshi enthusiastically and diligently worked to enrich and perfect the entire system of karate techniques, with the cooperation of his third son Gigō Funakoshi, as well as Shigeru Egami and Motonobu Hironishi. One of their achievements was to institute the Ten no Kata to be used as a sparring form and the Taikyoku no Kata.

Shigeru Egami, the author of this book, learned karate under both Master Funakoshi and Gigō Funakoshi. He and Gigō Funakoshi were the men who established the basic principles for Shōtō-kan karate, so that karate ideals and techniques could be passed on faithfully and correctly.

In this book, the author expounds the importance of first developing a supple body and cutting down on waste of energy, and only then concentrating one's spiritual and physical energies on the perfection of the techniques of attack and defense.

In its clear and concise explanation of the fundamental techniques of karate, this book presents photographs that show exactly how techniques developed to their present form. It is thus a most valuable source of information, useful not only for beginners who wish to learn and practice karate, but also for instructors who can use it to check their own standards, and for researchers as well.

It is fervently hoped that the people who seek to learn the way of karate will not be satisfied simply with acquiring the techniques through physical training, but, through perfecting the *kata* ("formal exercises") and the *kumite* ("sparring forms"), will attain a level of harmony far beyond mere physical combat.

Many more people practice karate than did when this book was originally published, among whom there are now numerous women. This is entirely in keeping with Master Funakoshi's teaching that karate is a fighting art open to anybody, whether old or young, male or female.

JŌTARO TAKAGI
PRESIDENT OF THE JAPAN KARATE-DŌ SHŌTŌ-KAI
PRINCIPAL OF THE SHŌTŌ-KAN

A Note from America

Following Master Gichin Funakoshi in the world of Karate-dō is Senior Shigeru Egami. I feel that we of the next generation are fortunate to have this man.

For those who see the light of truth in the simple sentences of this book, the reward will be substantial, for I know that they are the ones who have practiced honestly for many years. To the beginner, the meaning will not be so readily apparent, since he has not had the direct experience of training to prepare him for it. If, however, he comes to appreciate the significance of hard training, and particularly the importance of developing a supple body, he will benefit greatly. With time, as he trains under a good teacher, he will achieve deeper understanding.

For those who are peering into the darkness for peace on earth, especially those who are seeking enlightenment through the martial arts, Senior Egami has indicated the direction in this book. In the future, there will be no dichotomy of Eastern understanding versus Western understanding: there will be only the human being's understanding. At present, that time seems far away.

As one who has hoped to be a span in the bridge between East and West, I am highly honored to have the opportunity to write this note from America.

TSUTOMU OHSHIMA
SHOTOKAN KARATE
OF AMERICA

Preface

Forty years have passed since I began to practice karate under Master Gichin Funakoshi. During those years, I have of course changed physically and mentally; in some cases, l became aware of the changes myself, but at other times they were pointed out by others. But always, I think, they were inevitable. Moreover, there have been great changes in the techniques and the kata during this period. My objectives in writing this book are to review the changes that have taken place in Karate-dō—for the purpose of casting a fresh light on what is important in karate training—and to present the fundamentals to be practiced by the student.

The changes have by no means been merely technical ones; changes have also occurred in the way of thinking. We were taught, for example, that all movements follow a straight line and practiced in this way, but the truth is quite the opposite: karate movements never follow a straight line. Some movements are circular, some are up and down, and some are lateral. Although there was a time when we would have thought it inconceivable, even striking is not done in a straight line; it can be done in a number of ways. Blocking techniques have also changed, and the movements performed in a kata, from beginning to end, have become varied and flowing.

Since the changes are numerous and fundamental, several questions arise. For example, did the karate-ka of former days think of training in the fundamentals as the way leading to real practice? That is, did they realize that through practice they could clarify the relation between mind and body, understand the relation between one's own mind and the mind of another, and seek the innermost secrets of the human being?

The ideal of Gichin Funakoshi, who has come to be recognized as the "Father of Karate-dō," was to advance from *jutsu* ("technique") to *dō* (the "way"). It became my mission to realize this ideal, but here again questions arise: What is the meaning of "from technique to the way?" Through what kind of practice can one attain this ideal?

Karate-*jutsu* or Karate-*dō*? The distinction between the two must be clearly grasped. Karate-*jutsu* must be regarded as nothing more than a technique for homicide, and that, most emphatically, is not the objective of Karate-*dō*.

He who would follow the way of true karate must seek not only to coexist with his opponent but to achieve unity with him. There is no question of homicide, nor should emphasis ever be placed on winning. When practicing Karate-dō, what is important is to be one with your partner, move together, and make progress together.

The differences between the karate of today and that of former times extend even to warming-up exercises, for if the way of thinking changes, everything will change. Stress is now placed on suppleness of both mind and body. For those of us who began the practice of karate long ago, the result of making our bodies rigid was to become muscle-bound, and our power was dispersed to many parts of our bodies. The present concept is that the body be relaxed, supple and strong, and the power concentrated in one point. Furthermore, the mind should be clear, that is, without thoughts, and all movements should be made in a natural way. Without a clear, supple mind, the body cannot be supple.

That karate has come to be identified in the public mind as an "art of homicide" is indeed sad and unfortunate. It is not that. It is an art of self-defense, but in order to attain its benefits, the practitioner must be completely free of any egotistic feeling. This widespread, public misconception was very much in my mind while I wrote, and I would be very happy if this book could serve as a corrective to the mistaken public image and thus become a valuable guide to those who will practice karate in the future.

In 1972, at the request of Mr. Tomoji Miyamoto of the Japan Karate-dō Shōtō-kai's secretariat, I began a series of articles under the title "Changes in Technique" for *Karate-dō*, the newsletter of the Shōtō-kai. On the recommendation of my colleagues, and also in commemoration of my sixtieth birthday, these articles have been translated to form the basis of this book. Since I am not a writer by profession, I fear that this book is full of defects. However, I would like to dedicate it to the members of the Shōtō-kai in deep appreciation of their long friendship and support. I would also like to take this opportunity to express my heartfelt gratitude to the many persons who have been of assistance in bringing this book to publication.

Introduction

When Gichin Funakoshi came to Tokyo in the early 1920s, the art of karate was virtually unknown outside of his native prefecture of Okinawa. His purpose in making the trip was, at the invitation of the Ministry of Education, to give a demonstration of the art, and his intention had been to return to Okinawa. This he did not do, however, because of the advice he received from Jigorō Kanō, the father of judo; Hakudō Nakayama, a great authority on *kendō*; and others.

Having decided to spread Karate-dō (the Way of Karate) throughout Japan, he endeavored to do so with determination and enthusiasm, but not without difficulties. The number of students who came to him for instruction was very small at first, with the result that he lived in poverty and had to do a great number of odd-jobs simply to make ends meet. Who would have thought in those days that the popularity of this art of self-defense would spread beyond Japan to all parts of the world?

I recall trips that we followers of Funakoshi made to the Kyoto-Osaka area and the southern island of Kyushu under the leadership of Takeshi Shimoda, our instructor and the most talented among Funakoshi's students. That was around 1934, about twelve years after the master had given that first demonstration in Tokyo. Karate in

1. Gichin Funakoshi and Takeshi Shimoda

those days had the reputation of being merely a way of fighting, but it did have an aura of secrecy and mystery. Consequently, it would appear that what attracted capacity crowds to our demonstrations was nothing more than curiosity.

Although I am not familiar with the details of Shimoda's career, I understand that he was an expert in the Nen-ryū school of *kendō* and also studied *ninjitsu* (the art of making oneself invisible). In one of those unfortunate twists of fate, he became ill after our demonstration trip and died soon afterwards.

He had been acting as Master Funakoshi's assistant, teaching us when the latter was busy, and his place was taken by the master's third oldest son, Gigō, who was not only a man of excellent character but one highly skilled in the techniques of the art. There was no one better qualified to instruct the younger students. However, since he was working as an x-ray technician at both Tokyo Imperial University and the Ministry of Education, he was understandably reluctant to take on this additional task. After being strongly urged by both his father and the students, he finally agreed, and he soon won our admiration as well as our respect. I still remember vividly how we used to call him *"Waka Sensei,"* meaning "young teacher," to differentiate him from his father, whom we then called *"Rō Sensei,"* which means "old teacher." [Used in this way, *rō* has none of the not-quite-complimentary, or even derogatory, overtones that the English *old* might imply.] (It should be noted that Gigō was also called Yoshitaka, which is another way of reading the two characters that make up his first name.)

2. Gigō Funakoshi

Like Shimoda, Gigō Funakoshi died in the prime of life, while still in his thirties. That was in the spring of 1945, and I feel that he must have died of a broken heart. During the early years, Master Funakoshi had been without his own dōjō, but finally in the spring of 1936, the Shōtō-kan Dōjō was completed in the Mejiro district of Tokyo. Then in March, 1945, there was a great air raid in Tokyo (of course, there had been many others), and that splendid dōjō went up in flames. It had required the efforts of a great many people, not the least of whom had been Gigō. Already in the hospital at the time, it must have been too much for him to see that cherished dream destroyed.

At the present time, karate is being practiced in many countries throughout the world; in fact, it is riding the crest of a wave of popularity. But what is the meaning of this phenomenon? What is so attractive about this art of self-defense? Why do people practice it? What is their objective?

That Takeshi Shimoda and Gigō Funakoshi died at such an early age was a great loss for the world of Karate-dō. If they were still alive today, what would they think of the present situation?

The karate practiced today is quite different from that of forty years ago, and the number of styles now is said to total nearly one hundred. Many schools send instructors abroad to propagate their respective techniques. While it can be said that there are certain groups in the United States and Europe that, with the objective of understanding the soul of the Orient as a means of counteracting the impasse arising from materialistic civilization, place emphasis on the spiritual side of karate, the sad truth is that many styles teach only the fighting art and neglect the spiritual aspects. And the practitioners themselves, who offer lip service to the spirit of the art, have as their real objective the winning of matches. They speak of fostering an indomitable spirit, which in itself is praiseworthy, but we have to think of the results if this spirit is improperly used. As in the case of a hoodlum or madman wielding a knife, gun or other weapon against innocent people, the results could only be disastrous.

The present situation, then, is that the majority of followers of karate in overseas countries pursue karate for its fighting techniques, and it must be admitted that the proclivity to engage in combat is no less common in humans than in other animals. It is extremely doubtful that those enthusiasts have come to a full understanding of Karate-dō.

Mention should also be made of the negative influence of movies and television on the public image of karate, if not on the art itself.

Depicting karate as a mysterious way of fighting capable of causing death or injury with a single blow or kick and thus appealing to man's fighting instinct, the mass media present a pseudo art far from the real thing.

Gichin Funakoshi was an advocate of the spiritual aspects of Karate-dō and placed much greater emphasis on this than on the techniques of fighting. Moreover, he always practiced what he taught. If he were alive today to see what is happening to Karate-dō, what would he think? Those of us who are adhering strictly to orthodox karate as an art of self-defense must do all in our power to see that it is practiced in the proper way and that its spiritual side is understood to the fullest extent.

In striving for the mistaken, homicidal objective, the beginner will give his all in training, believing that compromise simply does not exist. To him, it is a simple black-and-white question of life or death; according to this view, one must either kill his adversary or be killed himself.

To kill with one blow or to emerge from a match or fight always victorious are objectives that only a beginner can seriously believe in. Never losing does not mean always winning. When one comes to a true understanding of this, one will have graduated from the beginners' class. In a contest, it is natural for the strongest to be the victor, but a contest is only a contest. In Karate-dō, there is neither strong man nor weak man. The essence of the art is mutual cooperation. This is the ultimate in Karate-dō.

After a child is born, the first persons he comes into contact with are his mother, his father, his brothers, his sisters. As he grows, he makes friends with other children and comes into contact with his teachers. He begins to read books and learn about men of the past. As he matures physically and mentally, he meets many kinds of people, and he forms some idea of human society. Since a man cannot exist by himself, he also comes to appreciate the importance of human relationships.

The relevance of this to karate training and practice is that they are in reality ways of pursuing and exploring the essence of being human. Thus, for example, even if you should have a partner who is vicious and determined to injure you, this is fortunate for you. To know yourself, to know your opponent, to understand the relationship between the two: these are the true objectives of training.

Compassion and *consideration for others* are commonplace words, frequently used, but to put them into practice is exceedingly difficult. Before taking *any* action, it is of the greatest importance not only to take the other person's position into consideration but to understand it fully. In fact, in coming to a perfect understanding of the other's position you will achieve a unity with him, and words like *victory* and *defeat* will be seen to be meaningless. This is the real secret of karate—coexisting with your opponent. And when this is accomplished, the understanding that human beings were made to cooperate with each other will become your own understanding. Practice will never be complete until this state of mind is achieved.

Beginning in the training of one's body, practice continues with the training of one's spirit. Finally one realizes that body and spirit are not two things but one. This is true practice.

Training of the body is the subject on which I have concentrated in the present work, but I have also explained the preliminary stages of practice. (The distinction between training and practice is an important one, concerning which I shall have more to say at the appropriate time.) The importance of training the body lies in the fact that if one's body is tense and rigid, it is impossible to be spiritually sound and flexible.

One point I should like to underscore at this time is that when one begins, he should approach training with an attitude of acceptance, follow instructions wholeheartedly, and always give his best. At this point he should not worry about form or whether his body is tense or relaxed. It is best to act naturally and concentrate on learning how to make the most powerful and effective blow with the hands or feet. In this way, one will come to realize that the most effective techniques, whether offensive or defensive, obtain from being natural and flexible. The time for questioning and expressing one's own opinions will come later, after the techniques have been mastered.

"There is no offense in karate" are words that I heard Master Funakoshi speak more than forty years ago, but I found it difficult to understand their meaning, for I myself had thought that karate was to be used in actual fighting. He also used to say that "you should never raise your hand against your opponent first. Only when it becomes absolutely necessary should you raise your hand. And even then, your intention should not be to kill or injure your opponent but only to block his attack. If he continues, then you should take a stance that will clearly show that it would be best for him to stop."

Being at that time only about twenty years old and full of energy, I thought to myself, "What is this old man saying? Is he moralizing? Why doesn't he teach me the truth?" Thinking that he was only trying to keep his younger followers from acting rashly, I could not make myself follow his injunction. As my skill improved and I became more confident, I came to the conclusion that it would be nonsense for me not to take the initiative. After all, was there not also the saying that "attacking first is the best defense"?

I must confess that I did engage in several fights, which made me even more confident in my skill and immoderately proud. It was not out of modesty that I concealed the fact that I was practicing karate. I am ashamed to admit that in those days I was arrogant and, consequently, must have been disliked by others.

Eventually, however, I decided that I would follow the master's advice, at least to the extent of not striking a blow before the point was reached where there was no alternative, and then I would fell my opponent with a single blow. I would also take care not to let my opponent see what the blow would be like before it was delivered.

As a child, I had been a weak individual. It was through hard training that I came to have confidence in the strength of my arms, and it was through hard training that I further strengthened them and my body. It was through hard training also that I was able to overcome a number of illnesses that I fell victim to. But this was only because I was a young man in my mid twenties.

After graduating from college, I entered the civil service but became dissatisfied and went to work for a private company. Again unhappy with my job, I then opened my own business. Altogether I changed jobs more than a score of times. Although I cannot give a reason, the one thing I continued, and have continued all these years, was my practice of karate.

Partly due to my experience with various kinds of work and partly due to my becoming older and more mature, my karate training has changed, both in style and in content. It was when I was a little past forty that an incident occurred that made me realize that real training was not the mere polishing of techniques for fighting. I then began to seek an understanding of the spiritual aspects of Karate-dō.

While a friend and I were drinking one day, we were surrounded by a gang of about ten hoodlums, who were obviously looking for trouble. I immediately took a good look at these men who had suddenly become my adversaries and looked for an opening that would enable me to break through the encirclement. Soon, however, I asked myself what sense there would be in fighting. Win or lose, there would be no honor. Even if I won the fight, there would be a scandal and I would be the loser.

If in my younger days I had been in such a situation, I would have seized the initiative in order to attack first and take my opponents by surprise. This time, while remaining calm, I looked for a solution that would leave everyone uninjured. I am glad to say that I was able to dissuade the gang from fighting. It was then that I realized that I had been successful in disengaging myself from the world of fighting, though I was still convinced that my power and skill were of such a level that I would not lose to any young hood.

Soon after this incident, I underwent an operation for removal of part of my stomach, and then about a year after that, I underwent a second, similar operation. Since I lost the strength of which I had been so proud, I could no longer practice karate. Even more serious was the difficulty I had in making a living. I look back at that time, during which I was plunged into abject despair, as the worst period of my life. But then I recalled other words of Gichin Funakoshi, who had maintained that "karate practice must be such that it can be practiced by anyone, the old as well as the young, women and children as well as men."

With that in mind, I determined to see if I could practice while in such poor physical condition. The results were reassuring, for I found that I could do so by carefully selecting certain methods. Having met with success, I made up my mind to devote the rest of my life to karate practice.

It was about ten years after my second stomach operation that I suffered a heart attack, which left me in a very precarious state, literally hovering between life and death. I had the good fortune to recover, but for three or four years after that, my physical strength was reduced to that of a new-born baby. It was impossible for me to practice karate, but during this period I learned something of great value from my younger colleagues: the importance of good human relations, the value inherent in friendship and the opportunity of having heart-to-heart talks and the preciousness of assistance freely extended in times of need. In this lies the essence of practice in Karate-dō.

Words that I have often heard are that "everything begins with *rei* and ends with *rei*." The word itself, however, can be interpreted in several ways; it is the *rei* of *reigi,* meaning "etiquette, courtesy, politeness," and it is also the *rei* of *keirei*, meaning "salutation" or "bow." The meaning of *rei* is sometimes explained in terms of *kata* or *katachi* ("formal exercises" and "form" or "shape"). It is of prime importance not only in karate but in all martial arts. For our purposes here, let us understand *rei* as the ceremonial bow in which courtesy and decorum are manifest.

He who would follow the way of karate must be courteous, not only in training but in daily life. While humble and gentle, he should never be servile. His performance of the kata should reflect boldness and confidence. This seemingly paradoxical combination of boldness and gentleness leads ultimately to harmony. It is true, as Master Funakoshi used to say, that the spirit of karate would be lost without courtesy.

It is also true that there are few persons who can make a perfect ceremonial bow, but one who can do this has to a great extent mastered the art. In order to do so, he must be a man of good, rounded character. In recent days, I have rarely met anyone who could make a perfect bow.

While in karate practice the man who makes a perfect bow seems to be full of openings, quite the opposite is true; he leaves no openings, and it would be difficult in the extreme for his opponent to deliver an effective blow or kick. When performing kata, begin with a bow and end with a bow. Be neither arrogant nor servile. From beginning to end, perform the kata in a natural way with humility.

Without sincerity, the bow is meaningless. Rather than be concerned about its outward appearance, put your heart and soul into the bow; then it will naturally take on a good shape.

For the beginner, it is natural to wish to become as strong as possible. And if he continues to practice with seriousness in order to attain this end, he will eventually reach a state wherein there is great harmony between body and spirit. But there will be no arrogance, only gentleness, and he will even forget that he is a man of great capability. There is a saying that "the strong hawk hides its talons." It is like that. I myself would like to attain this state, but it is only recently that I have become aware of it.

Master Funakoshi was often asked for examples of his fine calligraphy, and one of the expressions he used to write down and present to others was, "Don't go against nature." These words, which have a deep meaning, he thoroughly intended to be a maxim to be strictly observed.

It is difficult to define *nature* in so many words. Sun, moon and stars are part of nature, as are man, existence itself and the movement of all things. Flowers blooming in the spring and leaves falling in the autumn are natural phenomena, as are a man's birth, his growing up and becoming old, and his death. Earth, water, fire, wind, snow and rain are part of nature, from which we have much to learn. But no matter how much one opposes nature, he does not have the slightest chance of winning.

In our physical movements, there are those that are natural and others that are not. Through practice, we can learn to differentiate between the two and also learn to acquire natural movements. We should also learn the power that nature has endowed us with and how to use it, for a man has a great deal of hidden power of which he is not aware. The example of prodigious feats of strength and endurance exhibited during times of stress, such as fires and floods, comes to mind. These are sometimes described as "superhuman," but is this really the case? Although the person who performed such a feat was not aware that he possessed such power, it is my conviction that such powers are the endowment of nature and can be developed by one who trains in earnest and with perseverance.

I would like to pose a very crucial question: If instead of opposing the movements of your opponent, you moved with him in a natural way, what would happen? You will find that you and he become as one, and that when he moves to strike, your body will move naturally to avert the blow. And when you become capable of this, you will discover a completely different world—one that you had not known existed. When you are as one with your opponent and move naturally with him without opposition, then there is no such thing as a first strike. The meaning of *karate ni sente nashi* ("There is no first strike in karate") cannot be understood until you achieve this state.

Through courtesy you will take a humble attitude toward your opponent in training and be grateful to him. Without this attitude, there can be no training in the true sense. But if your objective is to batter your opponent senseless, you cannot attain this state. In real training and practice, anger, hatred and fear are completely absent. It is important to know that one can harbor neither homicidal intention nor enmity, neither opposition nor resistance, against one's opponent. When you reach this state, you will become one with your opponent and you will be able to move naturally in line with his movements. This, then, is the objective, physically and spiritually, of training and practicing karate. But it is a state than can be achieved only through strenuous practice.

It has been said that when one passes the age of sixty, he will no longer be able to engage in real practice. When I first heard those words, about twenty years before reaching that age, I could not understand their meaning. Now that I have reached that age, I think I can understand to some extent. Deterioration in one's physical strength becomes conspicuous, and it is impossible to engage in the same type of practice as young people do. Movements themselves become sluggish.

Nevertheless, in thinking back on my forty years of practicing karate, I come to the conclusion that, as my teacher Gichin Funakoshi said, karate is a martial art in which anyone can participate, young or old, man or woman, everyone. As for karate and life, I would like to say that practicing karate is indeed life and life is indeed practicing karate. My wish is to remain young in spirit throughout my days. To build up my gradually waning physical strength, I would like to engage in preparatory exercises before actually performing karate practice. And this is the way that I suggest that those who would follow Karate-dō proceed.

Recently it has come to my attention that there are some divergences of opinion on the preliminary stages of practice. In this book, I would like to express some of my personal opinions, which I hope will be a valuable source of reference to all. And I hope your practice will be done with diligence.

I Preparatory

I Preparatory

Warming-up Exercises

Karate training and practice begin with warming-up exercises. They are important and should be practiced in a serious frame of mind. Their purpose is to make and keep the body and limbs soft and supple, for the human body is naturally soft and flexible. It is only with death that it becomes rigid.

Having used the terms *training* and *practice*, I would like to indicate what I wish to convey by each. By *training* (the Japanese word is *renshū*), I mean training of the body, and by *practice* (*keiko* in Japanese), I mean training of the spirit. Practice or *keiko* is important not only in the martial arts but in other cultural activities where the spiritual aspects are paramount, such as flower arranging and the tea ceremony. Rather than training in karate, I wish to emphasize practice of Karate-dō.

Among the exercises popular today are some that only build up the muscles or involve stretching or flexing the arms and legs in an unnatural way. These are to be avoided. The objective is to maintain or improve one's health, rejuvenate one's body and spirit, eliminate stress, and enable the person who practices them to concentrate body and soul in his daily activities. So long as the exercises soften muscles, joints, tendons and other parts of the body, they may be engaged in freely. The warming-up exercises selected and described here have been in use for many years and are still popular.

The beginner may find that when he performs the exercises for the first time his body aches all over. He should not be discouraged by this. Also, he should not force himself to overdo the exercises. Practice that is overly vigorous will prevent one from doing the exercises smoothly.

Warming-up may be done either individually or in groups. If the latter, it is a good idea to pair off with a partner and take turns observing each other to see that the exercises are performed properly.

3. Sit with legs to front   *4. Grasp feet with hands*

A repetition of each exercise ten times for a period of about thirty minutes should be sufficient for warming-up. One should always:

Relax, physically and mentally.

Take his time.

Perform the exercises in gradual stages.

Continue to breathe naturally.

These exercises are quite strenuous, but loosening the muscles will keep them from becoming stiff and old, and the whole body will be rejuvenated. Even the functioning of the brain will become more elastic.

1. While sitting on the floor, stretch both legs out in front of you, keeping them close together. Do not bend your knees. Bend forward until your chest touches your legs and grasp your feet with your hands. This exercise should be continued until you are able to bend your body freely (figures 3 and 4).

2. Spread your legs and sit on the floor as shown in figure 5. Be careful not to bend your knees. Bend your body toward the front leg and grasp your foot with your hands (figure 6).

Repeat, facing in the opposite direction and bending toward the other leg.

5. Sit with legs spread

6. Grasp feet with hands

7. Crouch and extend one leg

8. Grasp foot with hand

9. Reach over head and grasp foot

3. From a standing position with the feet apart, bend one knee until the foot of that leg is firmly planted on the floor and extend the other leg straight out to the side (figure 7). Your hips should be almost touching the floor. Take care not to bend the knee of the extended leg. Bend toward the outstretched leg and grasp the foot with your hand (figure 8), or with both hands. Also practice grasping the extended toes with the opposite hand, with your arm reaching over your head, e.g., grasp your right foot with your left hand as shown in figure 9.

Repeat by extending the other leg and practicing in the other direction.

10. Sit and spread legs

11. Bend to side

12. Reach over head and grasp foot

13. Bend forward

4. Spread your legs to the sides as much as possible and sit on the floor. With sufficient practice, your legs will form a fairly straight line (figure 10). From this position, twist your body to the left or right (practice alternately) and (1) bend your body with your arms extended (figure 11); (2) bend your body and grasp the foot with the opposite hand (right foot with the left hand, as shown in figure 12, or vice versa).

Also practice bending straight forward with arms extended and touching your head to the floor. With practice, you will be able to touch the floor with your chest and stomach as shown in figure 13.

14. *Sit with soles together*   15. *Bend forward*   16. *Bend forward (side view)*

5. From the previous sitting position, bring the soles of the feet together (figure 14). The heels should be ramrod stiff, and the knees must touch the floor. (The beginner may find this difficult; he may press the knees down with his hands.) Bend forward with arms extended straight out (figures 15 and 16). Repeat until you can bend deeply.

6. Lie on your stomach. Grab your legs with your hands. Lift your head and chest and at the same time raise your legs with your hands (figure 17). With sufficient training, you will be able to touch your head with your feet.

7. Take a kneeling position with the knees close together. Then sway your body backward, keeping your hands against your sides so that the knees stay together (figure 18).

17. *Grasp feet with hands*   18. *Bend backward*

19. Front kick

8. Stand with your right leg slightly behind your left. Without bending the knee, kick upward with your right foot (figure 19). Practice until your knee touches your chest. This exercise should be practiced slowly at first and the tempo gradually increased.

Repeat with the left leg.

9. Stand straight with your feet together; then bend your knees and crouch. Simultaneously straighten your knees and kick with your right leg. The knee should be kept as straight as possible while kicking (figures 20 through 22).

Return to the crouching position and kick with the left leg.

10. First stand straight with the feet close together; then flex the knees slightly, as shown in figure 23. Kick sharply and repeatedly several times without stopping (figure 24).

Do the same thing with the other leg.

11. Stand with your feet close together and then take a crouching position (figure 25). Utilizing the spring of the ankles, knees and hips, jump as high as possible. Simultaneously kick to the front with both legs, using the momentum of the jump (figures 26 and 27).

Alternatively, kick to the sides by opening the right and left legs simultaneously, as shown in figure 28.

20. Crouch

21. Raise knee

22. Kick

23. Flex knees

24. Kick

26. Jump

27. Kick to the front

25. Crouch

28. Kick to the sides

29

29. Crouch, feet outward   *30. Jump*   *31. Return to original position*

12. There are a number of ways to practice the rabbit hop. One way is to turn the feet outward and jump utilizing the spring of the knees and hips as shown in figures 29 through 31.

You may also practice the rabbit hop by keeping the knees together and jumping with the ankles, knees and hips.

A third way is to spread the knees, push your abdomen forward, and jump as shown in figures 32 through 35. In this case the power comes principally from the hips.

When doing this exercise, clasp your hands behind your back. Avoid the temptation to put your hands on your knees, because hands and knees will counteract each other.

Continue jumping. How long you will be able to continue in one practice session is a matter of will power. I suggest that you continue practice until you can rabbit hop for a distance of from one and one half to three miles.

Do not become tense while performing this exercise.

32. Crouch, knees apart   *33. Straighten up*   *34. Jump, abdomen forward* *35. Return to original position*

36. Crouch

37. Jump and bend backward

38. Yoga handstand
(*front view*)

13. Start the backward bending jump from a crouching position with your hands to the front. As you jump, throw your hands high above your head, thrust out your stomach, and bend your body backward, as shown in figures 36 and 37. Return to the original position.

This should be practiced in a relaxed state of mind and body.

14. For the yoga handstand, kneel and bend forward so your elbows and forearms are on the floor (figure 39). Slowly raise your trunk and legs to a vertical position, as shown in figures 40 through 42.

Your entire body must be relaxed. Eliminate all tension from mind as well as body. As in the other warming-up exercises, do not stop breathing.

39. *Kneel with elbows on floor*

40. *Raise torso*

41. *Raise legs*

42. *Yoga handstand*

43–48. *Exercising with a partner*

Doing exercises with a partner is beneficial in itself but will also indicate to what extent your body has become flexible.

Sitting with your legs extended to the sides, let your partner stand behind your thighs and press your back down (figures 43 and 44). Or sitting with your soles together, let him press your back down (figure 45).

Standing back to back, relax and let your partner grasp your hands and bend forward (figure 46).

Facing your partner directly (figure 47) or sideways (figure 48), raise your leg and rest it on your partner's shoulder. Practice with both legs.

49. *Hold pole in front* 50. *Raise pole* 51. *Lower pole*

To relax the whole body, practice the following exercises using a pole about six feet long and one to one and one half inches in diameter. Practice these in a relaxed mood, taking care not to overextend yourself.

1. Hold the pole in front of you with the backs of the hands to the front. The hands should be a little more than shoulder width apart (figure 49). Without bending the elbows, slowly raise the pole above your head (figure 50).

Up to this point, one should experience no difficulty. Now gradually lower the pole behind your back without changing your grip, as shown in figure 51. In order to do this, all strength must be eliminated from the shoulders.

52. *Back view*

Reverse the process, raising the pole slowly above your head and lowering it to the original position.

This exercise must be done slowly. Performing it quickly can result in injury to the shoulders.

Once you can perform this exercise smoothly, narrow the distance between the hands and continue to exercise. In this way, you will come to understand the significance of the relationship between mind and body. After you have mastered it, practice the other exercises with the pole for relaxation of the whole body.

53. Hold pole in front

54. Bring right foot over

55. Raise left arm

56. Lower left arm

57. Bring right foot over pole

58. Original position

2. Grasp the pole with both hands and hold it in front of you (figure 53). Raise your right foot and bring it down over your right arm, so that your leg is between your arms. This is shown in figure 54.

Without bending the elbow, raise your left arm above your head (figure 55). Then crouch and lower your left arm to a level below your hips (figure 56). There should be no strength in the shoulders.

59. *Raise pole*   60. *Lower pole in front*

The pole is now behind the left knee. Raise your right foot and bring it back over the pole (figure 57).

Now go through the reverse movements to return to the original position (figure 58).

Repeat from the other side.

3. Hold the pole behind your back with the backs of the hands outward. Raise the pole over your head (figure 59). Do not bend the elbows. Then bring it down in front of you (figure 60).

Seiza

One of the first problems the beginner will encounter is sitting in *seiza*, but I hope you will learn to appreciate its significance in the practice of Karate-dō. While it is impossible to give a literal translation of the word in English, the essence of *seiza* is to sit with a straight back in a clean atmosphere with a clean conscience and meditate in silence.

In the dōjō, it is permissible to sit with the knees a little apart, but in a more formal situation, the knees should be kept tightly together. It is unfortunate that *seiza* has sometimes been used as a form of punishment, for this is a completely wrong practice.

You may begin practice of this form of sitting by spreading your knees as widely as possible (figure 62) and then gradually closing them. Since by doing this repeatedly you will understand the meaning of it, I will refrain from explanation.

It is most important to keep your back absolutely straight. Your shoulders must not droop, nor must your chin protrude. The feeling is that of being suspended from a taut rope that makes it impossible to bend your back even slightly. You must never be tense. The tip of your nose should form a vertical line with your navel. This is the ideal physical form of *seiza*.

Sit silently with your mind clear and chaste. For this purpose, you should choose a clean and chaste place, for as a human being, you will naturally be disturbed by noise. Choose a quiet place; sit quietly and correctly. Do not close your eyes completely; it will not do if you fall asleep or even doze off.

Fix your gaze on a spot about three feet in front of you but without staring. This may seem paradoxical, but the objective is not to look outward but into your own self. (One way to achieve concentration, sweep away idle thoughts and induce calmness is to fix your gaze on one spot in the room.)

The idle thoughts that may come into your mind at first will disappear in time. This may happen again, but eventually they will disappear completely. Then your mind will be very quiet and chaste. You should continue practice in *seiza* until you can sit in this style for about one hour.

61. Seiza

62. Seiza, *with knees widely spread*

63. Seiza (*side view*)

64. Seiza (*back view*)

II Fundamentals

II Fundamentals

Traditionally, there have been three types of karate practice: fundamentals, kata ("formal exercises") and kumite ("sparring"). Moreover, the term *fundamentals* has been defined in a number of ways, ranging from the inclusion of all aspects of practice to being limited to three, or two, or even one. However, the various definitions are not themselves of great concern at this point.

In truth, the kata are everything, and insofar as practice is concerned, they may be thought of in terms of (1) fundamentals and (2) kumite, fundamentals being representative movements and techniques of the kata selected for practice, and kumite being techniques practiced with a partner, i.e., application of techniques. Among the kata, of course, are easy ones and difficult ones, and representative kata may be designated as fundamental and practiced at an earlier stage than others.

In the present instance, I have followed the traditional division as a matter of practicality.

As I have already stated, karate techniques have undergone a number of changes in the forty years that I have been practicing karate, and these changes extend to all aspects of training. When I began training, the body was kept almost rigid and the karate-ka stood almost upright when taking a stance. The crouching style adopted later was still not as low as the stance we take today. The reason for the low stance is to relax tension in muscles not being used and to test the limits of one's capability.

I am often asked whether a low stance is suitable for combat. It must be borne in mind that the low stance is for practice purposes and that one must be able to make agile movements even from a low stance. It is only the amateur who thinks that a low stance is not suitable for combat.

There was a time when the most important thing was to imagine in one's mind every conceivable combat situation and train one's body so as to emerge victorious. The second most important thing was to test, through practice, whether each movement would be effective in actual combat. This is no longer the case. Now the objective of practice is to transcend mere victory or defeat and arrive at a state where you and your opponent are as one.

If karate as a whole is thought of as the polishing of techniques in preparation for actual combat, the karate-ka will be able to train his body to be supple and strong. This will lead to the fostering of a strong and supple mind. Then, body and mind will become as one, and the karate-ka will be able to fight at his best. But having accomplished this, the karate-ka will be able to transcend the fight and become as one with his opponent. One enters a realm where he and his antagonist do not exist as separate, individual entities; it is a world beyond egotism.

To return to the matter of the low stance, if one harbors the idea that it is inappropriate for combat, he is not in a proper state of mind to practice. The instructor may be in the habit of saying only "Do this," or "Do that," but he has good reasons for conducting practice in the way that he does. The beginner should follow instructions faithfully and, for the time being, keep his opinions to himself.

On encountering a difficult fundamental, you may decide that it is impossible to perform it. In such a case, the only course to follow is to practice repeatedly; in time you will succeed in mastering the difficult fundamental. Thinking only of yourself will prevent you from discovering the real essence of practice. As a first step to casting away your ego, you should listen to what your instructor says and practice accordingly. This should not be thought of as following blindly, for, as you progress, doubts will come to mind and you will question the way of doing certain things. But this too is practice.

Stances

Stances that have come down from former days are: the natural stance (*hachiji-dachi*), the reverse natural stance (*gyaku hachiji-dachi*), feet-together stance (*heisoku-dachi*), horse-riding stance (*kiba-dachi*), back stance (*kōkutsu-dachi*), cat-leg stance (*nekoashi-dachi*), front stance (*zenkutsu-dachi*) and the so-called hourglass stance (*sanchin-dachi*). Two stances that were adopted in more recent times are the square stance (*shiko-dachi*) and the immovable stance (*fudō-dachi*).

Natural Stance (*Hachiji-dachi*)

As its name implies, this is the most natural of all karate stances. It is also called *shizen-tai*, the literal meaning of which is "natural position." It is the basis for all other stances, which can be regarded as variations of it. When taking this stance, one should be in complete harmony with nature and with the universe.

It was once the custom to take a rigid stance, with all the muscles hard and alert (figure 65), but this was really quite the opposite of a natural position.

Place your heels so that they are separated by a distance roughly equal to the width of your shoulders with the toes turned slightly

65. *Old natural stance*

66. *Natural stance*

outward. All tension must be eliminated from hands, legs, knees, hips, stomach and shoulders. Stand in a natural position, relaxed and silent, as if your whole body were fused with the atmosphere. This stance is shown in figure 66.

Although it may seem easy, the fact is that this stance is difficult in certain respects. From this position, you must be able to vary your stance according to changes in your opponent's stance. For the beginner, this may be difficult, so you must practice shifting to various positions, taking as low a stance as possible.

"Be calm of spirit but quick of mind." The meaning of these words is, I believe, that one should always be cool and calm while at the same time being attentive to everything around him. If you are to cope with an opponent, this is the frame of mind you must be in when you take the natural stance. This is the reason for regarding all other stances as being variations of this one. Of course, the other stances must be practiced faithfully too.

Feet-together Stance (*Heisoku-dachi*)

From the natural stance, slowly bring your feet together until they touch each other (figure 67). As you do this, consider the meaning of the stance; in comparing it with the other stances, think and feel how it is different and how the body has changed.

Formerly, as shown in figure 68, the legs were tense, but now the knees though straight are relaxed.

67. Feet-together stance

68. Bow from old feet-together stance

Horse-riding Stance (*Kiba-dachi*)

The difference between the present stance and the older, rigid stance, shown in figure 69, can be seen in the effects of fatigue. It used to be that as one became tired, his body tended to rise. Also breathing was irregular. Now, breathing is natural, and as one becomes tired, his stance becomes lower and the knees buckle. Although the way pain is experienced is different in the two cases, the present form is quite as gruelling as the former one. I advise you to experience this pain.

While in the feet-together stance, open your feet to form a ninety-degree angle (figure 70). Then pivoting on the front part of your feet,

69. *Old horse-riding stance*

70. *Open feet* 71. *Reverse natural stance*   72. *Pivot on heels*   73. *Horse-riding stance*

open the heels. This is the reverse natural stance (*gyaku hachiji-dachi*) shown in figure 71. Pivot on your heels and move your legs further apart, into a stance similar to the natural stance but with the feet more widely separated (figure 72). Again pivot on the front part of your feet, moving your legs further apart. The distance between the feet should be adjusted according to the trainee's body structure.

Once the feet are in place, twist the knees towards the toes as much as possible and drop your body as low as possible. The feet should be firmly fixed, the toes opening outward and the heels pressed inward. All unnecessary muscular tension should be eliminated from body

74. *Horse-riding stance*
    (*side view*)

and legs. If too much strength is put in firming the legs, the knees will tend to open. To prevent this, apply strength from the outside of the knees. The objective of tightening the legs is to stabilize them.

The upper part of the body should be perpendicular to the ground, leaning neither to the front nor to the rear. Place emphasis on bending the ankles as much as possible while keeping the upper part of the body as natural as possible. This is the horse-riding stance, shown in figures 73 and 74.

Square Stance (*Shiko-dachi*)

The distance between the feet is the same as in the horse-riding stance. The difference is that the feet are turned outward at ninety degrees, and the hips are lower. While keeping your spine straight, thrust out your stomach. Bend your knees deeply. This is shown in figures 75 and 76. It will be instructive to compare this stance with the horse-riding stance. You may practice moving forward in this position. (This is similar to the *suri-ashi* of *sumō* wrestling.)

Back Stance (*Kōkutsu-dachi*)

If you move forward from a low natural position, your body, lead by your head, will tend to lean forward. To prevent this, bring one leg forward lightly while simultaneously bending the knee. Also deeply bend the supporting leg, which is the center of gravity. Unless the ankle is soft and flexible, it will be difficult to bend the knee, causing your backside to protrude and your body to lean too far forward. The upper body should be kept straight, stomach thrust out and hips low (figure 77).

Cat-leg Stance (*Nekoashi-dachi*)

In this stance, the body is twisted a little from the natural stance so that you meet your opponent in a half-facing position (*hanmi*), with the legs in the position shown in figure 79 and the hips low. This stance can also be taken from the back stance by withdrawing the forward foot just before reverting to the natural stance. The center of gravity is, of course, the rear leg. Whether the rigidity of the former stance (figure 80) was to prevent one from being kicked off balance or to make a more effective kick is an ambiguous point. However, from my experience, it is best to relax the body.

75. Square stance

76. Square stance (side view)

77. Back stance

78. Back stance (front view)

79. Cat-leg stance

80. Old cat-leg stance

Front Stance (*Zenkutsu-dachi*)

In the old front stance, the rear leg was kept straight, and the navel was pointed squarely at the opponent (figure 81). The stance was very cramped; eventually it was abolished as a result of discussions between Master Funakoshi and his son Gigō. However, many karate-ka still adhere to and practice this old form. And while it is not practical, it will enable one to strengthen his ankles. From this point of view, it may be a good idea to practice it.

Later the form changed from one in which both feet turned inward to one in which the front foot pointed straight ahead. And the rear leg instead of being kept straight was bent as it is in the immovable stance.

In the present form, shown in figure 82, the body is not rigid but relaxed, and the body weight is shifted toward the front leg. The knee of the front leg is bent deeply, and the knee of the rear leg, naturally and only slightly. The distance between the feet is about three feet. For the beginner, the distance between the axis of the front foot and the heel of the rear foot will be four to six inches, but with practice, the heel of the rear foot and the axis of the front foot will form a straight line directed toward the opponent. The toes of the back foot should be pointed forward and slightly to the inside; those of the front foot may be pointed slightly to the outside.

As in all stances, the upper body is straight.

Comparing this with the horse-riding stance, the body is turned

81. *Old front stance*

82. *Front stance*

completely sideways, the weight concentrated on the front foot, and the shape of the tips of the feet is changed. This is a very demanding stance and should be practiced diligently, as we were required to do in the old days.

This front stance is a variation of the immovable stance and is very effective for punching when you have to lunge forward and strike with all your might.

Immovable Stance (*Fudō-dachi*)

After extensive study, the immovable stance was developed to replace the old front stance, which was not useful for actual combat. But even after the stance changed, the body was still kept rigid (figure 83).

In the present form, the rear leg is bent slightly, the stomach is thrust out, the hips are as low as possible, and the center of gravity is in the middle. All parts of the body are relaxed. This stance is a natural one for forward and backward movement in a low position. This stance is shown in figure 84.

In reality, stances are not fixed and immobile; performed in a series of movements, they are fleeting.

From a front stance, one might return to a natural stance simply by bringing the rear foot up to the front foot. But let us take an example from striking. When you strike, the form of the legs goes through a

83. Old immovable stance

84. Immovable stance

85. *Front stance*

86. *Bring back foot in line with front foot*

87. *Immovable stance*

88. *Front stance*

series of stances: front stance, immovable and front stance, as shown in figures 85 through 88. This continues until both feet are brought together in the natural stance. Or if the opponent withdraws, you would not bring the feet together but pursue him by advancing one foot.

Hourglass Stance (*Sanchin-dachi*)

In this stance, which is not currently practiced by the Shōtō-kai, the feet were formerly further apart than they are in the present form (figure 89 and figure 90, respectively). In another old form the feet were even more widely spaced. It used to be considered necessary for the fostering of *kongō-mi*. There are some who practice this stance today, but I feel they have mistaken the true meaning of *kongō-mi*, *kongō-shin* and *kongō-riki*. [*Kongō* means "diamond," while *mi*, *shin* and *riki* mean "body," "mind" and "strength." A literal translation does not give the full significance, however, for they are Buddhist terms. As an example, *kongō-shin* signifies the single-minded will of the bodhisattva to aspire to sublime ends.]

Since this is a stance handed down by pioneers of the art, I believe it is worthy of consideration and study as the trainee makes progress in his practice.

89. *Old hourglass stance*

90. *Hourglass stance*

Offensive Techniques

In actual combat, there are only two alternatives to consider: to take the offensive or to be on the defensive, but from the offensive, one may go on the defensive, and from a defensive position, one may go on the offensive. Thus it can be said that "defensive equals offensive." There are no other alternatives, for to run away means death.

Life is no different. Some men think that life is not only a battle but a battle in which they must take the offensive to carve out their destiny. Other men are more conservative and passive and think that it is better not to oppose destiny. In any case, there is no escaping life, which is in certain respects a series of battles. It may also be said that the choice of offensive or defensive depends on the character of the individual.

Considered as a fighting art, the techniques of karate can be divided into two categories, offensive and defensive, In general, offensive techniques include striking, kicking, punching, jabbing and throwing, but karate practice usually consists of only striking, punching and kicking. For the future, it might be well to reconsider throwing techniques (*torite* or *nagewaza,* figures 91 and 92).

Hard training is necessary to learn kicking and thrusting techniques; with sufficient practice, however, the karate-ka will be able to master the state of mental preparedness, timing and rhythm required for

91. Throwing technique

92. Throwing technique

their execution. Since this is a fighting art, an opponent is necessary, so one will find himself on the defensive at times.

"To transcend combat" is an expression deep in meaning and difficult to understand. There are those who interpret it superficially and look down on karate as a fighting art. The beginner should disregard such an interpretation and practice as if he were engaged in deadly combat. Karate-dō should be understood as an art in which life or death is the result of a single error. It may be long afterwards before one understands *to transcend combat,* or *to transcend life and death.* It would be foolish to decide prematurely that one has grasped the essence of Karate-dō in its entirety.

The question remains of what form kicking and striking will take—more than that, the real nature of offensive and defensive techniques—once one understands the meaning of *to transcend combat.* It may be said that only with an understanding of those words will one understand the techniques and forms. It may even be said that it is not to late to understand the forms after one understands this expression. And if one understood *to transcend life and death,* the way of kicking or striking would be drastically different from what the beginner has in mind. However, understanding is likely to take time. It is best to practice hard, for in this way, one learns with the body as well as the mind. Deeper understanding will come eventually.

So I would repeat what I said with regard to the warming-up exercises: cast away your thoughts and opinions, follow your instructor, and train diligently. Without understanding combat, one cannot expect to understand transcending combat. Practice with the intent of felling your opponent with a single blow or a single kick.

Kicking

Front Kick (*Mae-geri*)

The form of the foot in the front kick when I began practice was with the toes folded down (figure 93). The part of the foot that struck the opponent was the first joint of the big toe. Since the toes had to be strong—otherwise they might be broken—we were made to practice standing, and even walking, with our toes folded, as shown in figure 94. Having mastered this, we practiced jumping with our toes in this position, and I was eventually able to perform a double kick (*nidan-geri*) in this fashion. Although this kick was performed in demonstra-

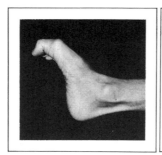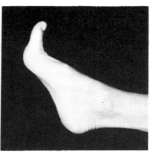

93. Old form of foot   *94. Walking with toes folded 95. Present form of foot*

tions because of its interest, it has no relevance to training, and few practiced it because it was so painful.

The form of the foot presently used is shown in figure 95. The toes are bent back as much as possible. No special training is required to form the foot, but to avoid breaking or spraining the toes, the kick must land squarely on the target. Where and how to aim the kick is a matter of long and careful study; diligent practice every day is necessary if you are to kick your opponent in the right place and from the right direction.

Of fundamental importance in the front kick is raising the knee as high as possible (*kakaekomi*), until it touches the stomach. Practice raising your knee as shown in figure 96.

96. Raising knee

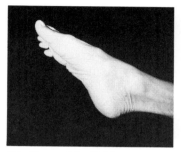

97. Toe used in kicking

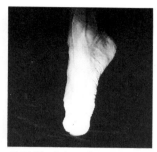

98. Training of toes

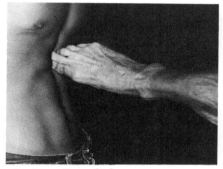

99. Roundhouse kick

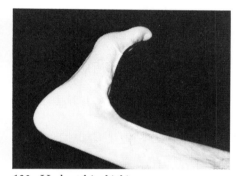

100. Heel used in kicking

Another way to make contact is with the tip of the big toe, although this is not practiced much today (figure 97). This is not feasible unless power is concentrated in the big toe. To strengthen the big toes for this purpose, one should practice standing and walking on them, in the manner of a toe dance as shown in figure 98. If one is successful in this, he will find that the power is considerable. A roundhouse kick (*mawashi-geri*) delivered in this way is very effectiye (figure 99).

The heel may also be used in kicking (figure 100). Although this is a style not practiced much today, I would advise practicing it, as it will be helpful when extending your feet backwards and forwards in the warming-up exercises.

Practice of the front kick should begin from the front stance (figure 101). With the weight on the front leg, kick with the rear leg. Emphasis should be placed on raising the knee of the kicking leg as high as possible. An understanding of the necessity for this should

101. Front stance

102. Raise knee

103. Front kick

104. Lower leg

105. Return to front stance

106. Front kick (front view)

come from your training. The front kick is shown in figures 101 through 106. Later, practice should be done from other stances: immovable stance, back stance, natural stance, and so on.

In addition to the part of the foot to be used, consider carefully the target area. In the front kick as in other kicks, there are the upper or face area (*jōdan*, figure 107), middle or chest area (*chūdan*, figure 108) and the lower area of the body (*gedan*). Directing a kick to a particular area of your opponent's body will not be possible, however, without an understanding of the raising of the leg.

107. Upper-level kick

108. Middle-level kick

Side Kick (*Yoko-geri*)

The two types of side kick are the side-up kick (*keage*) and the side-thrust kick (*kekomi* or *kebanashi*). There are far too many trainees who do not understand the difference between the two, so the problem of when to use one or the other should be studied carefully.

The difference between the present side-thrust kick and the old form is that now the heel is used whereas formerly we used the sword foot, i.e., the outer edge of the foot (*sokutō*, figure 109). In performing the Tekki Kata, we used to go from the *nuki-ashi* (figure 111) to the horse-riding stance using the sword foot. All the body weight was placed in the kicking foot. If we came down on the sole of the kicking

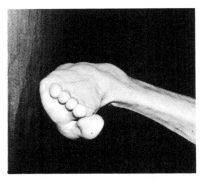

109. Edge of foot used in kicking

110. *Horse-riding stance*

111. Nuki-ashi

112. *Raise leg*

113. *Side-thrust kick*

114. *Horse-riding stance*

115. *Returning-wave kick*

foot, the shock stunned us. A forcefully executed kick with the sword foot could break a floorboard along its grain. I recall that when that happened, the younger Funakoshi would praise us, but the master himself would look displeased and say, "So, you've done it again. You're wrong." Still, if one perfected this sword foot, the returning-wave kick of the Tekki Kata (figures 114 and 115) was easy to perform, and the form itself was beautiful.

The side-thrust kick is performed as shown in figures 110 through 113, beginning from a horse-riding stance. First the left foot is brought

116. Natural stance   117. Front kick

118. Side kick   119–20. Back kick, with raised knee

lightly over and to the right of the right foot. Then the kick is
executed.

I recommend that it also be practiced from the front stance,
immovable stance and back stance, since this is closely related to
spreading the legs to the sides in the warming-up exercises.

You should practice until you are able to perform successively a
front kick, a side kick and a back kick from the natural stance, as
shown in figures 116 through 120.

Roundhouse Kick (*Mawashi-geri*)

A great deal of ambiguity seems to surround the roundhouse kick (*mawashi-geri*) and the crescent-moon kick (*mikazuki-geri*). They were practiced accurately as two types at one time, but nowadays it would seem that the crescent-moon kick is practiced instead of the roundhouse kick. In the early days, even the rather exotic name *mikazuki*, meaning literally "new" or "crescent moon," did not exist. My suspicion is that the crescent-moon kick was invented by someone who could not master the roundhouse kick and also had a distaste for real practice. Diligent practice of the roundhouse kick will show that the crescent-moon kick is nothing more than an application of the former.

As in other forms of kicking, study carefully where and how to kick. Otherwise this form will not be effective. On the basis of experience, I have found that this form is very effective when the tips of the toes strike the opponent in the solar plexus. When practicing alone, you may hang a small ball from the ceiling and kick freely in all directions.

Figures 121 through 124 show the roundhouse kick beginning from the front stance. Rather than using only a snap, concentrate on putting the whole force of the body into the kick. Basically, you should open your legs as wide as possible and kick horizontally from the side so that the foot strikes the target at a right angle.

121. *Front stance*   122. *Raise leg*   123. *Roundhouse kick*   124. *Roundhouse kick (front view)*

125. Front stance 126. Crescent-moon kick

127. Crescent-moon kick (front view)

Figures 126 and 127 show the crescent-moon kick.

As another form of practice, you may try executing the crescent-moon kick by changing from a front kick, simultaneously twisting your ankles and your hips and putting all of your body weight behind the kick.

Double Kick (*Nidan-geri*)

On instructions from Gigō Funakoshi, I practiced the jump kick from the immovable stance and eventually was able to attain a height of eight feet. I practiced this until I was about thirty-eight years old. When I was a little over forty, I set ten feet as my target, but after undergoing a stomach operation, I was unable to practice this. I wonder if there is anyone who would like to take my place and try for this height. If one fully uses the spring of the ankles, knees and hips, and practices long and faithfully, I do not think it is an impossible height.

This form of kicking takes its name from the two kicks that are performed while jumping; the first is aimed at the middle level (*chūdan*) and the second, at the upper level (*jōdan*), hence, *nidan*, or "two levels." The reason that this kick is little practiced today may be that it is considered impractical and somewhat dangerous. While it may be said that all kicks are dangerous, it must be admitted that the

128. Front stance

129. Middle-level kick

130. Return leg quickly

131. Upper-level kick

double kick leaves the kicker in a very unstable position, both while he is kicking in the air and after he has landed. The karate-ka who would practice this kick should have the attitude of putting his life on the line, or going for broke. Still, I recommend the double kick as a means to developing a supple body. Without making use of a running start, one should jump as high as possible. (Photographs sometimes give an exaggerated impression of the height of the jump, but showing off is not the objective. The jump kick should be practiced for its own sake.)

The double kick from the front stance is shown in figures 128 through 131. You should make your body as light as possible. When you finish kicking with one leg, kick immediately with the other leg, utilizing the natural reaction that comes from bringing back the first leg. Do not drop to the floor with a thump. You should land as softly as a cat. This will require long practice.

In practicing the double kick, bring back the leg after making the second kick and kick to the side before landing. This will help you to perform the double kick more smoothly. This variation might be called a triple kick, or *sandan-geri*.

It might also be interesting to perform a combination of the front kick and the roundhouse kick. In this case, do a front kick with one leg and follow it with a roundhouse kick with the other leg. This will be impossible unless your body is soft and flexible. A single error will send you sprawling on the floor. As far as that goes, tenseness will prevent you from doing the double kick at all. To jump-kick higher and with greater speed, relax.

Simultaneous Kick (*Sōsoku-geri*)

This is the jump-kick known also as *moro-geri*.

In practicing this technique, I used to turn my body sideways and kick at my opponent in an attitude of all or nothing (that is, go for broke), for one mistake would spell disaster. The meaning and objective have changed somewhat, so that now the emphasis is in making the muscles soft and flexible, enabling one to kick freely either to the front or to the sides. Using the momentum of rising and kicking is a natural way to strengthen the muscles of the back and inner parts of the legs.

Jump from a low crouching position and kick simultaneously with both legs. The kicks may be made either to the front or to the sides (figures 132 and 133). (The two ways of doing this are also shown in the warming-up exercises.)

132. *Simultaneous kick to front* 133. *Simultaneous kick to sides*

Techniques of kicking have become highly developed, and while I have not gone into great detail, I believe that I have indicated the fundamental changes.

In daily life, a man uses his feet and legs frequently, but there seems to be a reluctance to use them in any but the most ordinary ways. It is my belief that one should be able to use his lower limbs as readily as he does his upper limbs, and therein lies the reason that I myself have trained and practiced so hard.

I do not know the reason for the reluctance on the part of those who do not want to train strenuously. Do they think they will turn into monkeys? Of course they will not, and I advise them to train hard. Consider the advantage in being capable of striking your opponent in the face, deflecting his blow and kicking him in the shoulder with both legs.

Because of training faithfully in the double kick, I actually escaped from a fight by jumping over my adversary's head. This was not, as some people wanted to believe, a triangular-jump (*sankaku tobi*). It was only the application of a double kick. The triangular-jump is a much more complicated and higher-grade technique.

At any rate, practice whatever technique you want to, putting body and soul into your practice. The result will be that in an emergency, you will execute the technique very naturally. Train hard, practice hard, and someday you will discover that the fundamentals you have mastered will be of great help to you.

Striking

Striking is the life of karate, or so it has been said. Is this really true? Obviously, if karate is regarded as a fighting art, striking is indispensable. But beyond this is the self-evident fact that if the karate-ka does not have the ability to strike accurately, his adversary has no need for blocking techniques. In this sense striking is the life of the art. The beginner should think about this and give his all in practice.

Although there is the saying that "there is no offensive in karate" (*karate ni sente nashi*) and all kata begin with blocking, our training included striking from the very beginning. And a very offensive way of striking it was. As I remember, kata were practiced from the time Gichin Funakoshi introduced karate in Tokyo; I do not recall, however, when and for what reason striking came to be taught from the start of training. (This is a problem needing further study.)

Striking from the natural stance was practiced first. When this was mastered, we practiced from the horse-riding stance and were made to repeat the same technique hundreds of times during a single practice session, which might last thirty or forty minutes. Our fists were tightly clenched, and our armpits closed; we put power in our stomachs and tensed our legs. The training was extremely strenuous, and, in those days, rather abnormal and not good for the health.

We were always told to take a low stance, but as practice continued our bodies would naturally rise, and the power would seep from our muscles, despite our best efforts. With more training, we were able to keep a low posture without much effort, and although the sweat poured, our breath came in gasps, and our muscles were rigid, there was a feeling of exhilaration from having developed our bodies to a fine state of fitness. With our faces taking on an eaglelike sharpness and not an extra ounce of flesh, we considered ourselves real budō-ka.

The use of the fist has changed drastically. In those days, striking was different as applied in fundamentals, kata and kumite. There was a similarity between the fundamentals and the kata, but in a kata where the form and direction change, it was difficult to strike in accordance with the fundamentals. (But then performance according to fundamentals is still difficult.) In the case of sparring, particularly free sparring, a strike was quite different from the one seen in the fundamentals or in the kata. If an opponent stood up and became excited, the quality was altogether different.

A shortcoming of our practice was lack of serious study of such important elements of the martial arts as rhythm, timing and distance (*chōshi*, *hyōshi* and *ma no torikata*). Although we read about breathing (*kokyū*) and vital energy (*ki*) in books, they were not discussed, perhaps out of shame at our ignorance. Understanding the true meaning of these words was as difficult as trying to find a needle in a haystack.

Why, I wondered, was everyone practicing his striking as if he had full confidence in himself when actually his blows were ineffective? Conceit would seem to be the answer, since each man could easily believe that his punches were a little better than the next man's. If a man allowed someone to punch him in the stomach, for example, and the striker injured his wrist, the man could conceitedly think that if he had done the punching, he would not have injured his wrist because he had trained harder.

I came to realize that my way of thinking about power had been greatly in error, for power to me meant that of the body and of the arms. What I should have considered was the power of the body as a unit. We speak of body power and spiritual power. It was only when I pursued both that my striking began to undergo a change. The problem is that of complete harmony between body and soul.

After the Second World War, I went up to Tokyo and met some friends who took me to a karate dōjō. What I saw was very surprising. Both the movements and the forms of those who were practicing were on a small scale, unlike those of former days.

Then in 1952 or 1953, a former colleague demonstrated a very effective way of striking to me. I was astonished. The difference lay not in the form, which was little changed, but in the concept. In fact, it broke all precedents. I made up my mind to start all over again and practice with this new concept. My way of practice was completely altered, from stiff, Pinocchio-like movements to rhythmical ones. I succeeded only after months and months of study with the young karate-ka. The young men were making fast progress, and it was apparent that I had much to learn from them.

Among the problems I studied, and sometimes had to study over and over again, was how to avoid injury to the wrists, elbows and shoulders. The first realization that lead to a solution was that the human body, being a living thing, is very elastic. If power is concentrated in the wrist or the elbow or the shoulder, it will return to the place of concentration. If you spread out your elbows or raise your shoulder, power will escape from those places. It was once thought that the wrists could be trained by practicing the back fist (*uraken*), but this is not true.

To use the fist effectively, two points are crucial: (1) relaxing and (2) concentrating power. If the body is tense or rigid, the power in the elbows, shoulders, stomach, hips and legs cannot be released. Power cannot be dispersed throughout the body; it must be concentrated in the fist alone. I resolved to put this into practice. (The beginner will find it impossible to release power, for he has not learned to concentrate it, but concentration can be done quite naturally.)

Since he is unaccustomed to striking, the beginner will at first be confused. It is important not to put any power in the arm. Simply straighten your elbow naturally and take all power out of the arm and shoulder. Not only must concentration of the power be in the fist but the movement must not be impeded due to tenseness or rigidity.

There was a time when, to test the effectiveness of punches, I decided to lend my stomach as a target to others. Since I was mean looking and others thought that I would try something out of the ordinary, no one would lend his stomach to me. I knew that this way of testing was dangerous, but I decided to try it anyway, as there was no other way and I thought that the way of striking was not really effective. And this was true, even with karate-ka who had been practicing on the striking post (*makiwara*) for six or eight years. Because of putting too much power in the wrist, elbow and shoulder, the blows that landed on my stomach were already weakened considerably, and I felt no pain whatsoever. Moreover, the greater the concentration and the faster the blow, the greater was the impact on the wrist, which could result in a broken wrist.

The most important thing is how you feel. Practice as if your blow will pierce through your opponent or the striking post.

It was in early 1956 that I began to have some confidence that the way of striking I had been practicing was effective. I asked a colleague to let me punch his stomach. Since this was only a couple of months after my stomach operation, he refused, thinking that I did not have sufficient strength and fearing that I would open the incision. I was adamant and he finally agreed. Taking care to protect my own stomach, I thrust out my fist very lightly. To my amazement, the blow was very effective, and he dropped with a thump. You can imagine how elated and happy I was, knowing that my way of practice had not been mistaken.

Then in 1960, a foreigner who was a great karate enthusiast came to me and requested that I strike his bare stomach. A huge man, he had let other karate students punch his bare stomach without, he said, feeling any pain. I did not want to fell him, however, so I had him wrap a couple of cushions around his stomach. What I had in mind was to see whether my blow would pierce through his stomach and come out behind his back.

My first light punch did not affect him at all, but the second was different. "It went through!" he exclaimed. Later he reported that he had to get up to go to the toilet many times that night and averred that from then on he would "believe anything" I said.

The point is that the effectiveness of a blow cannot be discovered simply from its appearance. And herein lies one difficulty in practicing.

The Fist

An objective in studying striking techniques was to learn how to avoid wrist injuries. One result was that I changed the form of the fist I used.

Until twenty years ago, it was considered necessary to perfect the fists so that a good blow could be made with either one. The four fingers were folded tightly, and the thumb tightly gripped the first two fingers. The little finger was also tightly bent. But this was not sufficient. In the case of a beginner, the angle formed by the back of the hand and the fingers would not be less than ninety degrees. To achieve this, as shown in figure 134, one practiced with the striking post for months or even years.

Forty years ago, practice with the striking post was thought of as the basis of all karate training. The striking post was to be like a lifelong companion. We wanted to perfect fists that would withstand the shock of impact on any kind of object, no matter how hard the object or how hard we struck.

If you practice with the striking post, blisters will form on the areas of the hand that come in contact with it. The blisters will break and blood will appear. Later, the flesh will be torn and bone will appear. With further practice, calluses will form on the knuckles (figure 135), the area will turn black and blue, and the calluses will bleed from their bases. They will grow larger and larger and eventually unite to form one big callus as hard as or harder than the sole of the foot.

By this time, cartilage will have formed around the bone, creating a very hard fist. (I recall having my fists x-rayed and feeling very satisfied that this had happened.) Calluses will also develop on the palms where the fingertips touch. It took me more than a decade of punching the striking post to develop iron-hard fists, of which I was

134. Old regular fist

135. Formation of calluses

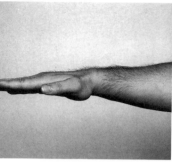

136–38. Forming single-point fist

proud. (But at the same time, I was rather ashamed to show my hands in front of members of the fairer sex.)

Another way to strengthen the fists that I would recommend is to practice doing handstands with the fists clenched. Or you may do push-ups with the hands clenched. These may be begun on a softer surface, such as tatami, and continued on a hard wooden floor.

As I said, after studying the technique of striking, I adopted a different form of fist. I made sure that the middle joint of my middle finger struck the target squarely. As shown in figures 136 through 138, the fist is made by tightly clenching the thumb and little finger. It is a rather ordinary fist that anyone can make, but it is the most effective and powerful. This is the form of the fist today, and practice with the striking post is no longer common. One precaution should be noted: when you twist your fist on contact, be careful that there is no unnecessary strength in the elbow or shoulder.

Practice from the Front Stance

Comparing the present and old forms, the difference lies in that we used to thrust out our fist as quickly as possible and did not change the position of our shoulders or hips. Consequently, the faster the punch, the more was the power that was required in the shoulder to stop it. This was not easy, but we found it could be accomplished by closing our armpits and putting power in them, as we were instructed to do. At first, the muscles in our armpits were not developed; it took months, or years, to satisfy our instructors.

To begin, extend your left fist so that it is directly in front of the body's median line and a little lower than shoulder height, with the

139. *Straight punch from natural stance*

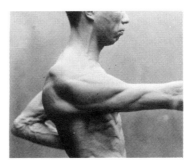

140. *Tighten armpit (striking arm)*

141. *Tighten armpit (withdrawing arm)*

back of the fist upward. The right fist is at the right hip with the back of the fist downward.

Simultaneously withdraw your left fist to your left hip and thrust out your right fist so that it arrives at a point in front of the body's median line, slightly lower than shoulder level (figure 139). This is for a middle-level strike, which is usual in practice today. For an upper-level strike, the position is on a level with the eyes.

Both arms are twisted during the movement, so that the back of the right fist comes upward and the back of the left fist comes downward.

Naturally, the shoulder will tend to follow the punch. At this point, you must hold it back by tightening the armpit, as shown in figure 140 You will find this very difficult. The armpit of the arm that is withdrawn must also be closed, and the forearm must be horizontal to the floor, as shown in figure 141. To do this, the shoulder must be forcefully dropped.

It is unnatural to stop a punch made with great force, but this is the correct way to practice. Eventually, you should be able to do this naturally.

Practice from the Horse-riding Stance

After you have learned to strike from the natural stance, practice from the horse-riding stance as shown in figures 142 and 143.

142. *Left punch from horse-riding stance*   143. *Right punch from horse-riding stance*

Practice from the Natural Stance

The practice of striking from this stance is similar to that from the natural stance or horse-riding stance, except that now you practice the so-called front punch and reverse punch. With your feet firmly fixed, practice striking with the arm on the same side as the advanced foot—front punch, figure 144—and with the arm on the other side—reverse punch, figure 145. Repeat this alternately, and, of course, practice from both left front stance and right front stance.

144. *Front punch*   145. *Reverse punch*

Striking

The foregoing explains the basic points of striking. Now I would like to discuss striking itself.

In the old style of practice, we started by taking the position for a lower-level block (*gedan-barai*) with the left foot and the left hand to the front (figure 146). Advancing the right foot, and just before it touched the floor, we thrust straight ahead with the right fist (figure 147). The fist is directly in front of the body's median line, while the shoulders are at a right angle to the line of progress. Of course, the left hand is withdrawn to the left hip, and the arms are rotated, so that the fingers of the right hand, which were up are now down, and the fingers of the left hand, which were down are now up. The stance shown is the old front stance, in which the body was rigid.

Many people, a great majority I would say, practice this by striking just after the foot has landed, but I and the followers of my school practiced in the manner described.

A description of practice with the striking post will be helpful in understanding the changes that have taken place and the technique of striking as it should be.

Taking the position shown in figure 148, one should have the feeling that the fist will pierce the striking post by a distance of seven or eight inches. While in a half-facing back stance, one fist is cocked at the hip, and the other fist is in the lower-level block position. Then, shifting the body weight from the back leg to the front leg, the navel comes to squarely face the striking post. The hips are twisted as the

146. *Lower-level block position*   147. *Right front punch*   148–49. *Striking* makiwara (*reverse punch*)

punch is delivered. This is shown in figure 149. We were frequently cautioned about bringing back the withdrawing fist as quickly as possible, so there would be more power in the striking fist. As I recall, this way of striking was the most effective, because the power was concentrated in one spot.

From the above, one should be able to understand the movements of the hands. It is also necessary to understand the movement of the body as a whole.

Figures 150 through 153 show the front punch executed from the front stance. When moving forward, the back foot is brought straight

150. *Front stance*

151. *Bring back foot in line with front foot*

152. *Immovable stance*

153. *Right front punch*

forward, and the tip of the big toe faces the line of progress. It is natural for the punch to be made when the foot goes forward.

This is the new way of striking. With the body relaxed, the body weight centered on the hips and legs, and the power concentrated in the fist, punch through your target or opponent. Your breathing must not stop during the execution. The greatest effect is obtained from the minimum of power.

As you advance, you will practice the front punch or the reverse punch, but some thought should be given to what this means. Consider, for example, striking from the immovable stance. If there is not much distance between your opponent and yourself, the punch will be a reverse punch; if the distance is greater, the punch will be a front punch. Thus while you practice front punch or reverse punch, the two are the same in essence. It might even be said that the front punch is the extension of the reverse punch.

As another example, take striking from the natural stance. Depending on your opponent's movements, you may simultaneously thrust out your right foot and hand, or your left hand and right foot, and so on. But what happens when your opponent steps back? Since you will have to strike anyway, you will have to change feet. Then you may use either a front punch or a reverse punch.

The significance of the present way of striking will become more apparent if we give further attention to the practices of the past.

It is not correct to say, as it was said at one time, that the reverse punch is effective but the front punch is not. As I mentioned previously, we first practiced the reverse punch beginning from a lower-level block position. The feet were firmly fixed, and it was called a reverse punch from a fixed position (*sonoba gyaku-tsuki*). This method was said to facilitate striking from the front stance as well as practice with the striking post. After this, forward and backward movements were practiced.

We did not know why the reverse punch was considered the more effective, but the reason is now apparent. In practicing with the striking post, it was easier to put all of the body strength into the blow. Moreover, the position changed from lower-level block to half-facing to facing the target squarely, with the hips turning. Consequently, we had the impression of the more body power, the more effective the blow.

It seemed to me that Master Funakoshi hit the striking post very lightly, uttering words that sounded like "*hoi, hoi.*" At that time, I thought that he was not striking forcefully and attributed it to his being small of stature and already about sixty years of age.

As for Takeshi Shimoda, he was not a big man either, and he kept a low posture; he did not seem to hit the striking post very powerfully. I was amazed to find out that he practiced a thousand punches with one fist every day, and when it rained, he would practice anyway, with an umbrella over his head. I was even more amazed when I was made to stand before him and receive his punch. Although his blows were light, I simply could not ward them off, no matter how hard I tried.

Gigō Funakoshi was about the same age as the trainees, and his blows were terrific. One thing I could not understand: While he told us to strike from the hips, he himself took a stance more like the horse-riding stance and aimed his blows at the striking post from a position with his hands dangling from his sides, without using his hips much. But there was no questioning the power of his blows as he lunged forward with all his body weight behind them. He frequently broke the striking post in two. With this as an example, we tried very hard to imitate him and practiced hard with the goal of breaking the striking post.

There was a difference in the way we practiced moving forward. The back foot was first brought alongside the front foot and then thrust forward, in an arc-shaped movement (figure 154), and the front foot was turned to the inside as shown in figures 155 and 156. The rigidity of the old-style stance and the delivery of the blow after the feet had become stabilized also contributed to the ineffectiveness of the blow.

154. Forward movement

155. Old form of foot

156. Old form of foot (front view)

At first it was very difficult to strike simultaneously with the forward movement of the foot. We say "simultaneously," but the foot must be thrust out with a certain momentum, and it would appear that one was jumping. I found that the way of thinking, though not mistaken, contained certain problems. What would be more natural would be to forget hand and foot and think about moving the hips and punching with them. Hand and foot will follow at the same time and in unison. Although I began to realize this only gradually, there was no mistake about the result.

The source of the problem had been the way of thinking, and the movement could not be done smoothly. At one time, we were taught to strike with hips and stomach; this was difficult, and only after a long period of trial and error could we do so. But we came to emulate the way of striking of Master Funakoshi, Takeshi Shimoda and Gigō Funakoshi. I still wonder why I did not understand their way more quickly.

The practice I have mentioned was conducted around 1935, which was about the time that the form and position of the sword-hand block (*shutō-uke*) was changed from sideways to half facing. Everything had been conceived in terms of actual combat, and after a series of studies, some changes were made.

The change of the form of the front foot when striking also changed the contents. This may be the most significant of the changes that I have mentioned.

The posture in all the stances became lower, and it was about that time that the immovable stance, which made movement very free, was created. This, a most extraordinary and excellent change effected only after long study of conventional stances, was a break with ancient tradition. Among the traditions were some that were not correct and were adhered to only because they were traditional. At any rate much courage was needed to break away and create new stances.

The old form of the front stance waned, was for a time used only to strengthen one's ankles, and has today been replaced by the new front stance. In this case, I think additional study might be given to the training of the ankles (see figure 81). There are karate-ka who have trained for three or four years and still cannot bend their ankles fully. Although this training can be done from the horse-riding or back stance, there are times when this is unsatisfactory, some trainees saying that their ankles are stiff and nothing can be done about it. I believe the old front stance would be more effective. We were made to practice it, and although it was painful and required great effort, we managed to do it.

At one time, I had confidence that my punches were effective. I could break boards, tiles and even bricks with my fists. With my back fist, I could shatter boards half an inch thick with one blow, and with my regular fist (*seiken*), I could break ten tiles piled one on top of the other without much difficulty. During practice, however, I found that a misdirected blow was virtually ineffective.

157. Breaking tiles

What astonished me was that even when I practiced with the greatest earnestness and with all my might, my blows and kicks were not effective. The shock of this discovery naturally led me to entertain doubts about the karate blow, which was said to be capable of killing a man even three or five years afterwards (*sannen goroshi* or *gonen goroshi*). I thought that since these words appeared in documents of the past, they must be true, and that there must be some deep secret to the lethality of the karate blow.

Pondering this, I began to search for the secret. I studied a lot of the literature and even took a trip to Okinawa to ask the opinion of veteran karate-ka there. But their answers were ambiguous, and I obtained not even an inkling of the secret. Although I allowed myself to be struck, perhaps more than ten thousand times altogether, I did not find a punch that was genuinely effective, except in one solitary instance.

In prearranged sparring, I was to make an upper-level strike and my opponent was to duck and hit me in the solar plexus. When he did, I felt the air leave my lungs. I became dizzy and thought I was on the verge of death. The blow must have combined rhythm, timing and distance (*chōshi*, *hyōshi* and *ma no torikata*); still, as I think back on that incident, it seems that the combination may have occurred fortuitously during the course of the sparring.

When I practiced, the figures of Master Funakoshi, of Takeshi Shimoda and of Gigō Funakoshi popped into my mind, and I could hear their words clearly, as if they were teaching me in the dōjō. I recalled how the master struck in a natural and light way, how Shimoda did it lightly but accurately, and how the younger Funakoshi did it so quickly and with such power, although his arms were dangling from his sides. I remembered, too, how I could not avoid the blow and how it hurt when it landed. I read *Karate-dō Kyōhan* again and again.

The conclusion I came to was that there was nothing to be done but to start anew and make a basic study of the difference between training (*renshū*) and practice (*keiko*). But how to proceed? This was indeed difficult to decide.

When I was about twenty years old, I went into the mountains and was taught swordsmanship by an old man, who was attired in the simple clothes of a farmer. I recollect clearly how he took the wooden sword from my hand and sundered the branch of a chestnut tree.

I recalled, too, practicing *aikidō* in my student days and judo and *kendō* in my middle school days.

I remembered how one of my seniors had advised me to stop karate and concentrate on the other martial arts, for, according to him, karate is a stiff fighting technique compared with the other martial arts.

The various types of martial arts that I studied fused as one in my body. Gradually, I came to understand the meaning of *dō*, or the "way." Among other things I came to appreciate was that taking a technique from another martial art and applying it in karate was futile. This can be done only by an accomplished expert, not a beginner.

Another important distinction that came to the surface was the difference between studying objectively and putting heart and soul in practice, between so-called learning and entering a dōjō not only to train but to practice, leaving one's body wholly in the care of his instructor. Thus I would like to emphasize what I have said before about the first thing in practice being to forget self. What is learned naturally during practice will make its appearance naturally afterwards. Changes will be not only physical but spiritual.

From reflecting deeply on the meaning of power, I came in time to realize that there is only one true objective. It also became apparent that I should not allow myself to be restricted to a small, dogmatic world.

Blocking Techniques

Blocking

Considering the changes in the way of striking, it is obvious that the way of blocking will also undergo changes. Our former blocking techniques would be very inadequate against striking techniques of the present day. If punches are not effective, there is no need for blocking, but with the development of effective striking, it was necessary to develop effective blocking techniques.

As a practitioner of a fighting art, the karate-ka must be prepared not only against other karate techniques but also against any type of weapon. And he must be prepared to defend himself against an attack from any direction, even while he himself is in motion. It is a mistake to think of attacks consisting only of striking and kicking. Thus, karate involves not only these but blocking and even grappling with an adversary.

It has been said that offense is the best defense. This is the ultimate objective, but it must be understood in a particular way. One can never simply wait for an opponent to attack. One must reach the stage where offense and defense become one. The techniques presented here are not simple ones for blocking only; from them one can instantly go on the attack.

Before we began to doubt the effectiveness of the way of striking, being struck frightened us out of our wits, for we thought that we might be killed. And although the punch delivered with a quick snap of the forearm lacked true power, it was painful, for our opponent had strengthened his forearm considerably by hard training on the striking post.

This was a case of power against power. Looking for a way to lessen the pain, we devised prearranged sparring for the practice of the lower-level block (*gedan-barai*) in order to strengthen our arms as well as our hands. The lower-level block was the only one we were permitted to practice, and we were made to continue until our arms were black and blue. It was excruciating for us as well as the ones who did the striking, since their hands would become swollen.

Yet our instructors did not let us rest, and young trainees were often reduced to tears. At that time, this type of training was considered the best way to make a man tough; we called it "baptism." We submitted unflinchingly, believing that our instructors were trying to turn us into good karate-ka, both physically and spiritually.

After our hands and arms returned to a more normal state, we were different persons. Even if struck hard, we did not feel much pain. It also became apparent that our hips were strengthened. And we were stronger in spirit. We ended up thinking that our seniors had been kind to train us with such severity.

This type of hard practice continued until after the Second World War, but it seemed to me that the lower-level block that reverberated to the hips was little practiced. And due to the lack of training of the hips, the way of striking was weak. We were astonished when a man whose punch had been blocked with a lower-level block was sent flying several paces backward. But this, after all, is the original function of the block.

There are various ways of thinking about blocking techniques. It goes without saying that one should imagine various situations that might arise in actual combat. Beyond that, one may ward off a blow passively, or he may take a more positive attitude and block while in an attacking position. I made it a rule to block by attacking as soon as my opponent began to strike, hitting him in the stomach immediately after the block. I knew from actual combat that this would make the block more effective.

It is necessary to study form and movement. In this respect, it is well to remember a key point with regard to striking: It is only when there is no feeling of power or resistance that the blow is effective. One may feel dissatisfaction with this, but since karate is a martial art, true technique does not require power. This is the reason why it can be practiced by anyone regardless of age. If one does not become self-complacent, he can practice even when he becomes very old or when his physical condition deteriorates.

Most important, be natural. Be relaxed, not rigid, and concentrate your power on the spot where you will block your opponent's punch. The matter of avoiding rigidity in the stomach and hips should be understood in terms of concentrating the body weight in them. When feet and arms move in unison with the hips, it is impossible to strike or block only with the arms or feet, a fact that has been proved by actual experimentation. Herein lies the difference between the present method and the old.

To block, it is first necessary to discover the opponent's intent.

Study the movements of his hips, legs and hands from this point of view. You may advance to a higher level by grasping the flow of your opponent's mind.

It is important to study rhythm, timing, distance and breathing, but nothing special need be done to acquire them. Understanding will come through practice. Similarly, I would advise the trainee to savor such expressions as "to know rhythm," "to grasp distance," "to sense timing," and so on, but their real meaning will only be revealed as a result of training and practice. As I mentioned before, it is fundamentally important to move with one's opponent.

Two other points should be kept in mind. The impression gained from photographs or watching actual practice is that techniques are performed in a fixed way. This is not quite correct. The forms, selected from a series of movements, have been fixed purely from necessity, as a convenient way of instruction.

The second point: Blocks may be divided into upper level, middle level and lower level (*jōdan, chūdan* and *gedan*). This may be interpreted to mean blocks against upper-level, middle-level or lower-level strikes or kicks. But it may also be interpreted in terms of blocks against any other strikes or kicks. Before practicing the blocking techniques, it is best to decide which meaning you will select.

Lower-level Block (*Gedan-barai*)

This is the first blocking technique to be practiced. It looks easy, but actually it is difficult. If you learn to do this well, you will be able to learn the other blocking techniques, because the fundamentals are the same.

Changes that have gradually occurred in the lower-level block involve the direction of the feet and the movement of the hips and body. We used to use the momentum of the rear leg when leaping forward, and although we were told to use our hips and stomach, they were not actually used to any extent. When the block was completed, the body was, of course, rigid. It was impossible to block because the punch stopped before it was completed.

One point that I think has not been studied sufficiently, to rectify the previous thinking and training methods, is the movement of the body. It seems to me that emphasis is still placed on blocking with all one's might. Against the present way of striking, this will be ineffectual, and the block may even be made to rebound. What is necessary is to anticipate the direction of the strike before blocking.

Thinking that it would take too much time and make the block too late, we did not appreciate the significance of bringing the blocking hand up to the opposite shoulder. It can be understood in this way: Suppose the opponent is induced to strike. His punch is then blocked with a downward sweeping blow. By this time, he is very close, and one can retaliate with a body blow. At the same time, there should, of course, be no unnecessary movements or forms, and one should practice to eliminate all of them.

Begin practice from the natural stance, first extending the left foot forward, bringing the left fist up beside the right ear (back of

158. *Natural stance* 159. *Raising hands*   160. *Left lower-level block*

161. *Forward movement*   162. *Right lower-level block*

the hand outward), and thrusting the right fist straight forward with the back of the hand upward (figures 158 and 159). Simultaneously withdraw your right fist to the right hip (back of the hand downward), step forward with the left foot, and bring your left fist down sideways to a point about six inches above the left knee. Be carefull to move the left hand and foot together and to have the left hand come into position at the same time that the foot touches the floor. You should then be in a half-facing position; the stance may be either the front stance, as shown in figure 160, or the immovable stance. Execute the movement in a rhythmic flow without stopping.

Continue by advancing, alternately practicing left and right blocks (figures 161 and 162). Also practice blocking while moving backward.

A left lower-level block may be used against an attack with the left fist (figure 163) or the right fist (figure 164). Various points of contact are shown in figures 165 through 168.

163. *Lower-level block against left punch*   164. *Lower-level block against right punch*

165–68. *Points of contact*

169. Left lower-level block

170. Left lower-level block-attack

171. Left lower-level block to right reverse punch

172. Left lower-level block to right front punch

173. Left lower-level block to throwing technique

From a lower-level block, counterattacks can be delivered in a number of ways, as shown in figures 169 through 173; of course, many other variations are possible.

The old-style lower-level block was done in a motion that was more like striking than sweeping and with the hand clenched. In actual practice, it was discovered that the block was more effective with the hand open, although this would not necessarily be true in all cases. I advise practicing with the open hand as shown in figures 174 and 175. Most karate-ka do it in this way today, particularly in sparring.

174. Block with open hand (wrist straight)   *175. Block with open hand (wrist bent)*

Why should it be more effective? The reason, I believe, is that making the fist causes some rigidity in the arm. With the hand open, the vital energy (*ki*) penetrates to the fingertips, making the block more effective.

I learned this valuable lesson in an unfortunate way. I arranged with my partner to block his punch lightly with my open hand, so as not to injure him. The result was that one of the bones in his forearm was cracked, for which I naturally apologized profusely, my intention having been just the opposite.

Upper-level Rising Block (*Jōdan age-uke*)

After the lower-level block, we were taught the upper-level rising block. From a left lower-level block position, the left fist was raised from under the right armpit, followed a half-moon shape, and stopped in front of the forehead, thus protecting the face. The fist did not go outside the line of the face, and the back of the fist was toward the face. As one moved forward, the stance became the old front stance, with the navel squarely facing to the front. When the block was completed, the movements of the body as a whole were stopped, but with practice, it became important to bring the blocking hand back to the hip.

After learning this, we practiced the block in the natural stance and also practiced moving to the front and to the rear. The purpose was to sweep an upper-level punch upward or sideways, or to get

176. Upper-level rising block

177. Ready position

178. Right front punch

179. Counterattack to neck

close to the opponent to strike his neck and shoulder (figures 176 through 179).

When moving forward the left hand was twisted and brought back to the hip at the same time that the right hand, tightly clenched, was swept up strongly. After the block, the hand was opened and the opponent's hand was grasped and pulled to the hip.

The present way of practicing the upper-level rising block is shown in figures 180 through 183. From the natural stance, take a left lower-level block position; then as you move forward with your right foot, raise your arms and block.

The two hands cross in front of the face, as shown in figure 181, the blocking hand taking an inside route and the withdrawing hand an outside route. This movement should be studied thoroughly. Think of the situation in which you are confronted by several opponents and must block punches one after another and then find an opening for your own attack.

The stance now is the immovable, rather than the front stance. However, if you leap forward toward your opponent, you will shift your weight forward and take a front stance.

180. *Natural stance*

181. *Crossing of arms*

182. *Raising arms*

183. *Upper-level block*

No power is put in the block, as it was formerly. The important thing is to see that the power of your opponent's punch does not come in full contact with your block. You should change the direction of his punch and block it without feeling any resistance. This can be learned through frequent and regular practice. Theory alone is not sufficient; you must learn with your body.

Beginners should make their movements as large as possible; if they make them small, they will find it difficult to improve. But eventually, all unnecessary movements and power must be eliminated.

I would advise that during practice sessions you picture in your mind the various situations you are likely to be placed in and consider your own methods of practice. Since the present striking techniques are different, it would be impossible to block with only the techniques of former days.

When he was more than eighty years of age, Gichin Funakoshi remarked that he was finally able to understand what an upper-level rising block is. That is how difficult the technique is.

Middle-level Sword-hand Block (*Chūdan Shutō-uke*)

There was a time when the sword-hand block was made from a sideways position (*mayoko*; see figure 197). After extensive study, Master Funakoshi found that the sword-hand block was more effective if executed in a half-facing position. That must have been about forty years ago.

From what I have heard, the sideways position was very difficult to take during actual combat, but it may be that the study of it has been insufficient to test its effectiveness thoroughly. In any case, it might be said that the technique was used for indirect rather than direct results. There have been those who have claimed that the sword-hand block was only a link to adjust the shape of the kata.

The form of the sword-hand block that we used to practice is shown in figures 184 and 185. We were taught that the hand and forearm should form a straight line and that the block should be made with that portion of the arm below the elbow. The hand itself was like the tip of a sword (figure 186).

The stance for this block is the back stance. From a natural stance, (figure 187), bend your knees fully and drop your body low. Placing all your body weight on the back (right) foot, bring the left foot

184. *Crossing of arms*

185. *Old middle-level sword-hand block*

186. *Sword hand*

187. *Natural stance* 188. *Open hand above shoulder*

189. *Left middle-level sword-hand block*

190. *Left middle-level sword-hand block (front view)*

forward lightly. Standing virtually on one foot, keep the upper torso evenly balanced (leaning neither to the right or left) and flex the front leg only slightly. (From this position, you could kick at any time.)

As soon as your left foot is brought forward, open both hands; thrust your right hand out lightly, and bring your left hand above your right shoulder, palm upward (figure 188). Bring your right elbow to your right side and your right hand in front of your stomach; thrust outward with your left arm. Be careful that the elbow

does not face outward (figure 189). The four fingers should be straight and close together and the thumb bent as shown in the photograph.

The movements and forms should be elastic, and except for some rigidity in the forearm, the body is relaxed. The only power necessary is that required to lower your hips and move your hands and feet. Even if the position is maintained for a long time, the body should not be rigid; if it is, the muscles will become stiff and lose their elasticity.

Having thoroughly practiced the form, the next thing is to practice the forward and backward movements. To continue, the right foot is brought alongside the left foot and the right hand is raised above the left shoulder. The right foot is brought forward, and the right hand is brought downward and sideways, while the left hand is brought in front of the stomach. The left hand should be ready to deliver a counterblow. (Changing from a left middle-level sword-hand block to a right spear-hand thrust is shown in figures 191 through 194.) Practice until you can do forward and backward movements freely.

This practice though difficult and exhausing is important and should be performed with diligence. A point not to be overlooked is that it is useful in making your ankles flexible.

A change of more recent origin (dating from six or eight years ago) is the shape of the hand. Instead of having the fingers together, they are all spread and the hand is curved upward. Consequently the shape of the entire arm is changed. The significance of this is that

191–94. Left middle-level sword-hand block to right spear-hand thrust

the power of the block is greater, and your opponent can be struck with greater force. This is shown in figure 195. You can also block with your wrist bent (figure 196).

It should be remembered that all techniques start and end in the natural stance. This is the true form of the techniques, I believe. Consequently, one must not stop in the position in which he has made the block.

To return to the matter of the two positions, sideways (*mayoko*) and half-facing (*hanmi*), I would like to express my personal opinion. I believe that there are reasons for their use and that they have their

195. Blocking with fingers spread

196. Block with wrist bent

197. *Sideways position*

198. *Half-facing position*

199. *Cat-leg stance*

200. *Grasping arm*

201. *Throwing technique*

202. From block to attack

203. Blocking from outside inward

204. Blocking from inside outward

respective merits and demerits. In the days when striking was not effective, they were not effective, and hardly any karate-ka mastered them, nor were they seen in free sparring. It is said that they are ineffectual against the present way of striking, but let us take an example.

Supposing your opponent attacks and you are in the sideways position (figure 197). As your hand touches your opponent's arm, change to a half-facing position and deflect the punch (figure 198). As he continues his attack, take a cat-leg stance (figure 199). Then you could follow through by grasping his arm and throwing him, as shown in figures 200 and 201. Or even if you did not escape the punch, you could change its direction with the movement of your hips and body. It would be good if a beginner could do this.

The middle-level sword-block can be used to block from the inside outward (figure 204), outside inward (figure 203), or in a block attack (figure 202).

Forearm Block (*Ude Uke*)

It used to be that the movements of the hands and feet were virtually independent of each other, the block being made after the foot that was moved forward had touched the ground. This was true in other practice, too, of course, but it goes without saying that striking or blocking with only the hands is to be avoided; it will not be effective. Movements centering on the hips must be studied extensively.

There are two types of forearm block, as practiced in the kata, but since they are little practiced as basic techniques at the present time, there is some confusion about their meaning. The two types are: (1) the inside block (*uchi uke*), in which the forearm is brought from the inside to the outside, and (2) the outside block (*soto uke*), in which the forearm is brought from the outside to the inside.

Let us begin with the inside forearm block. To block with the left hand beginning from the natural stance, lower the body. While extending the left foot forward, bring the left hand under the right armpit, thrust the right hand forward, and while bringing the right fist back to the right hip, thrust upward and forward with the left fist. This is shown in figures 205 through 207.

The right arm is twisted: the back of the fist is upward when the arm is thrust out and downward when the arm is returned to the hip. The left elbow is bent slightly, the back of the fist is downward, and the thumb-side of the arm is used to block the opponent's forearm if he has attacked with his right hand. The height of the fist is about level with the shoulder. The stance is a half-facing front stance.

In practice, the inside block may be used in two ways, either to hook the opponent's punch toward oneself or to leap inside for the block-attack.

In any case, care must be taken so that the blocking fist does not go outside the line of the shoulder. This would require unnecessary strength, and could result in an ineffectual block.

Practice alternate blocking with each arm and blocking while moving forward or backward. It should be noted that the relationship between the feet and hands is very similar to the lower-level block (*gedan-barai*). Practice while advancing as shown in figures 208 and 209.

In the left outside forearm block, the fist is raised high above the head and swung downward from outside to inside, as if you were aiming at your opponent's face. The left fist is brought to about

205. *Natural stance* 206. *Forward movement* 207. *Left inside forearm block*

208. *Forward movement* 209. *Right inside forearm block*

shoulder level and to a point in front of the right shoulder. As in the inside block, the elbow is slightly bent, but it is the little-finger side of the arm that comes in contact with the opponent's arm. The right fist is thrust out and then withdrawn to the hip and twisted—from back of the hand upward to back of the hand downward—during the movement. Of course the hips are lowered.

210. *Natural stance*

211. *Forward movement*

212. *Left outside forearm block*

213. *Forward movement*

214. *Right outside forearm block*

The outside forearm block is shown in figures 210 through 212 and blocking while continuing to advance in figures 213 and 214. Blocking while moving backward should also be practiced.

In both the inside and outside forearm blocks, it is also necessary to practice with the forward foot and blocking arm on opposite sides (e.g., left foot advanced, block with right arm, figures 215 and 216). This type of movement occurs in the kata, as in, for example, Heian 2. Consideration must be given to the turning of the hips as well as the movements of the feet and hands, and movements of the hands alone must be avoided by all means.

215. *Middle-level sword-hand block*

216. *Reverse forearm block*

In either the inside or outside forearm block, there are two ways of blocking: your arm may come in contact with either the inside or the outside of your opponent's arm. If you block with your left hand and he strikes with his right hand, contact will be with the inside of his arm, as shown in figure 217. But if he attacks with his left arm, contact will be with the outside of his arm, as shown in figure 218.

As mentioned previously, you should imagine various situations and consider the changes in stance and in the movements of the legs,

217. *Contact from inside*

218. *Contact from outside*

219. Attack with blocking arm

hips and feet with regard to them. Not everything can be imagined, however, so it is also important to practice with a partner, particularly with regard to such matters as whether to block lightly or to jump into your opponent and attack him with the blocking arm (figure 219).

We practiced with the idea that techniques and movements had a stopping point, but perhaps this way of thinking is not adequate. More important is the principle of movement flowing from the natural stance at the beginning to the natural stance at the end, for forms and movements will always undergo changes according to the fluid situations that will arise. Thinking that a movement is a thing unto itself and has a definite end will lead to inflexibility.

Besides the foregoing, there are other blocking techniques that should be practiced, such as the palm heel block (*teishō-barai*) and the iron hammer strike (*tettsui uchi*). The former is shown in figures 220 and 221, and the latter, in figures 222 through 224. These two, and others, are not much practiced today, but they can be used. What is desirable is to select the most difficult techniques from the various kata and practice diligently until they have been mastered, for one must be prepared for any emergency. Faithful practice of the techniques will be of great value when performing the kata.

In practicing, greatest emphasis should be placed on the movements as a whole, with care being taken so that the movements of hands, feet and hips are not independent of each other (as I have pointed out

220. *Palm heel block*

221. *Palm heel hand*

222–24. *Iron hammer strike*

before). To build a body that is supple as well as strong, you must
train it fully.

Whether done slowly or quickly, movements should be liquid and
never stop abruptly. They should be, in a sense, movements without
beginning or end. It has been said that a technique has a definite end
and that when one completely finishes a technique, it has been a matter
of cause and effect, but I do not share this opinion. If, when your
movements are fluid, you have the feeling of having hit or blocked,

then the technique is a success in a quite natural way. This should be kept in mind when practicing.

Never stop your breath, no matter how hectic your movements become. At first it will come in gasps, but as you continue, it will return to normal and stay normal, no matter how vigorous your movements.

There are many things to be learned. For one thing, you should pay attention to the relation between the blocking hand and the hand that is withdrawn to the hip. And it is necessary to study intensively how to prepare for changes, what the Yin-Yang relations are, and what kind of effect or power the blocking hand has.

If movements are repeated two, three, four . . . many, many times, what is their significance? What is the significance of practicing forward and backward movements? What is the relation between hips and legs? These and other matters have to be studied until they are fully understood.

I once asked a great number of college students to write down their impressions of the sword-hand block, and I recall that there were very nearly as many different observations as there were students. But whatever the observation, the important point is that it be translated into practice. Using one's head alone, that is, just thinking, is futile. You must practice what you think. This is real practice.

Takeshi Shimoda once told us that if we did a certain thing we would profit greatly. He said that we should repeatedly clench and open our hands, spreading our fingers as wide as possible when we opened our hands, and when we clenched them, we should do it quickly. We were advised to do this as often as possible. He suggested this casually, without explaining the purpose.

I practiced this diligently, on my walk to and from school. I later realized that this exercise is intricately related to karate practice. I advise you to try it, although I also will refrain from giving the reason. You will find the reason by yourself.

The body and spirit are fundamentally one. If you train your body, your spirit will also be trained.

III Kata

III Kata

The nineteen kata designated for practice by the Shōtō-kan were: Taikyoku Shodan, Taikyoku Nidan, Taikyoku Sandan, Heian Shodan, Heian Nidan, Heian Sandan, Heian Yodan, Heian Godan, Bassai, Kankū, Tekki Shodan, Tekki Nidan, Tekki Sandan, Hangetsu, Jutte, Empi, Gankaku, Jion, and Ten no Kata (Omote and Ura; these and the Taikyoku kata were created by Gigō Funakoshi).

Little practiced today are Taikyoku Nidan and Sandan and the Ten no Kata. It is my belief that the Nidan and Sandan of the Taikyoku should be abolished and Taikyoku Shodan should be renamed Taikyoku no Kata. As for the Ten no Kata, taking into consideration the great changes that have occurred in the way of striking and blocking, I believe it would be better not to practice this until further studies have been made. This leaves sixteen kata to be practiced, and I advise concentrating on these. If one has the time, he might practice other ancient kata—but to do so for the purpose of being able to boast that one has "mastered" a great number of kata would be pointless. It is said that in former days a single kata was practiced for a minimum of three years. Think what this means.

A kata may be regarded as in integration of offensive and defensive techniques, but it is more than that. One should try to understand the spirit of the master karate-ka who created the kata, for it has a life of its own and requires five or six years to be mastered.

Even in the forty years that I have been practicing, the changes have been many. (It would be interesting to be able to go back in time, to the point when the kata were created, and study them.) The order of the movements and the shape of the kata have not changed greatly; it is the way of thought, based on the movements of the body, that has changed extensively.

Looking at a kata, as practiced today, as a whole, the movements from the beginning natural stance to the ending natural stance should be liquid and flowing, the performance should be beautiful and rhythmic, and the performer, full of vitality and radiating power. Body and spirit must be one entity, and the power must be con-

225. *Heian*

226. *Kankū*

227. *Jutte*

228. *Tekki Shodan*

229. *Bassai*

230. *Empi*

READY POSITION

104

centrated. Breathing must continue without interruption. In former practice, there used to be a pause between one movement and the next; now movement continues rhythmically, without pausing, and is fluid and flexible.

Appearances can be deceptive. Although the movements look weak, in fact they are not. When the body and movements were rigid and the power dispersed, the techniques looked strong. Actually it was only the performer who felt that his blows were powerful. The only satisfaction was on his part; that is, it was only self-satisfaction. The opponent did not feel the blow to be strong, and the practice of stopping movement was actually dangerous. It could mean death to the person who does it. A weak-looking, soft and relaxed punch in which the power is concentrated will pierce anything.

However, the techniques should not be practiced simply so that they can be performed in the kata. Since karate is a fighting art, each technique or movement, whether offensive or defensive, has its own meaning. The karate-ka should consider their meaning, how and why they are effective, and practice accordingly.

While the movements performed in a kata are continuous and rhythmical, they are sometimes done slowly, sometimes quickly. This is one of three essential points in karate: (1) light and heavy application of strength, (2) expansion and contraction of the body and (3) fast and slow movements in techniques. There is no point in using strength indiscriminately, nor does speed in itself have any meaning. One must understand the meaning of each technique, each movement and the kata as a whole.

In all the martial arts, there are certain common points, such as rhythm, timing, distance, breathing and the flow of vital energy, and these are implicit in the kata. But there is no necessity to practice, say, how to breathe, as a specific thing. The crucial point is the performer's attitude toward the performance.

The flow of vital energy is a more difficult matter, since extensive and definitive studies have never been completed. Nevertheless, I believe that one can master it by concentrating body and soul.

What is vital, or intrinsic, energy (*ki* in Japanese, *ch'i* in Chinese)? While it is impossible to give a definitive answer, it may be said that it is possessed not only by human beings but by all objects, animate and inanimate. It is said to be the energy that fills the universe. It is desirable to feel the flow of vital energy with one's own body. This can be accomplished by practice.

Telepathy and psychokinesis are subjects that have been studied in recent years in the United States, Russia and Japan. My belief is that since ancient times there have been persons who were in possession of such "supernatural" powers, and that among the budō-ka of old there have been some who were cognizant of and practiced such powers. It would seem to me that there are numerous cases where such powers have been exhibited.

But it is not for the beginner to expect to manifest such powers. This would be impossible. He may practice karate simply as a fighting art and he may strive to become as strong as possible, but the beginner will not even be able to differentiate between concentration and relaxation.

It is best to begin by practicing an easy kata, such as Taikyoku, in a group with someone giving the orders. Practice should be done ten, twenty, fifty, a hundred times without stopping. You will not be able to use your head much, but you should not expect to. At this point, you should practice strenuously without worrying about whether your body is rigid or not. Simply practice hard; that is all.

What will happen? In the case of young people endowed with great power and vigor practicing the kata in this way, they will after ten or twenty repetitions become exhausted, for there is a limit. Continuing to practice, they will become even more exhausted, to the point of not being able to stand up, their breath will come in gasps, and their vision will blur. Out of sheer exhaustion, they may wish for unconsciousness. But they should not stop. Continuing in this state, they will become like automatons and will be unable to concentrate any power in their movements. To put it simply, they will not know what they are doing.

At this stage, they will realize that their movements have become soft and natural. The mind is useless, but the movements will have been acquired by the body.

If practice continues, they may come to the stage where the mind is very clear and the movements of the body understood. Or they may simply forget everything and crawl on the floor. They may repeatedly lose themselves and find themselves until they discover that they feel greatly exhilarated. It is then that they will understand that they have fallen down, or fainted, from exhaustion. But even then, if a command is heard, they will react in some way, though not necessarily physically. At the same time, they will come to comprehend the relation between themselves and the person giving the orders, the relation between the performers, and the relation between mind and body.

The body movements and the flow of feeling will at first be very confusing, then they will become very quiet, and finally one will enter a state of tranquillity and concentration, and the breath will become regular despite the strenuousness of the movements.

It is not the beginner who will do this. Only after long practice will he be able to gradually approach this state. Only when the body is thoroughly trained will he be able to arrive at this state.

Do not limit the exercise of your powers to a low level. I do not think anyone really knows his physical power and capability. You may think it impossible to continue, but eventually you will come. to realize the great power of your body and mind. You should challenge that power until you actually do fall down.

This type of practice should be done with quick movements, for example, the Taikyoku kata in five seconds. But there is another type of practice I advise doing. Try performing the Taikyoku kata in three, five or fifteen minutes without stopping your movements. This will prove more difficult than doing it quickly.

It is natural to want to offer criticisms at this stage; indeed, it is only human. What must be kept in mind is that you are entering and challenging an unknown world, the world of practice, for which your present state of knowledge is insufficient. You must practice until your body understands. This is practice.

The practice of the kata should never be assumed to be a cut-and-dried matter. Consider, for example, the ready (*yōi*) posture in various kata—that of the Heian kata, of Kankū, of Jutte, of the Tekki kata and so on are all different. Why should this be? It is tempting to assume that the ready posture of all kata should be the same, but this is not the case. We may even ask whether in a martial art there is a fixed posture (*kamae*), or whether a fixed posture is necessary. This seems to have some relation to yoga postures, but does it have any relation to the mudras of Esoteric Buddhism?

According to the literature on the Chinese T'ai-chi Ch'uan, the shape of the ready stance in Jutte is an expression of the unity of Yin and Yang. How did this come about and what function does it have? I know that there are changes in function among the various kata, but I must confess that I do not know the reason, nor why they change according to the kata. This is one problem, and there are many others, that I believe must be studied more extensively in the future.

231–36. *Practice of kata using pole*

Among the various kata, there are some whose fundamentals have been clearly described. In fact, though, it is difficult to perform them according to the fundamentals. Despite a lack of complete understanding, one should not assume that the movements have no meaning or function. I advise performing the movements, thinking about them, and interpreting them in your own way, concentrating heart and soul. This is practice.

In the evolution of karate, there was also practice using a pole. You may try practicing the kata with a pole, as shown in figures 231 through 236.

In a sense, practice, whether done alone or in a group, is a battle against one's own self. There is a strong temptation to be lazy and practice leisurely. One should not be lazy; one should learn how to accept hard practice. One should not think of practice as a fight against an opponent. He should challenge the extreme limits of his own strength.

IV Kumite

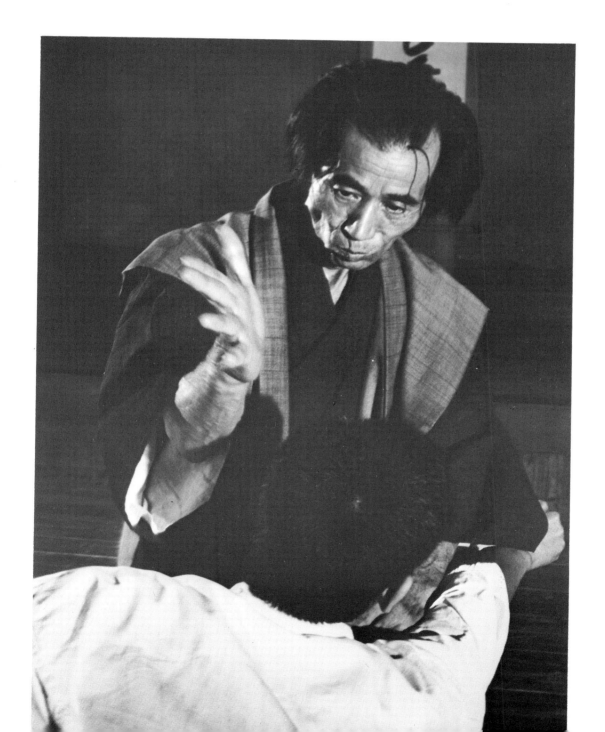

IV Kumite

Sparring (*kumite*) is the form of practice that has the most direct appeal not only to the beginner but to everyone who has any interest in karate. Everyone wants to start sparring practice as soon as possible, and it is for this reason that they practice the fundamentals assiduously. In my own case, I cannot forget the feeling of exhilaration I had when first permitted to practice sparring.

Perhaps the urge to fight in human beings is innate, but whether this is true or not, the feeling is well known. When one faces an opponent, he can hardly stand still. Blood rushing to the head and heart pounding, he is like a fighting cock raring to do battle. To intimidate his opponent, he wears a fierce scowl on his face, and he is full of fighting spirit.

At any rate, when one is finally allowed to practice sparring, he feels that he has at last become a full-fledged practitioner of the art; his happiness knows no bounds.

In the early days of modern karate, practice was concentrated on the kata and training with the striking post, emphasis being placed on training of the spirit through training of the body. It would seem that sparring began with the selection and practice of certain techniques from the kata. Before it was revealed by Gichin Funakoshi, and later adopted as a form of practice, it appears that masters of dōjō would, after a student became proficient in the kata, teach sparring, but only on an individual basis and in great secrecy.

Thus, sparring was originally a method of practice, not one to decide victory or defeat. It was practiced only to confirm whether a strike or block was effective or not. Although karate is a combat technique, sparring was not for actual combat nor was it a contest.

In ancient days, what we would now call a *contest* was a battle to death. To the man seeking the true way of the warrior (*budō*), a "contest" meant that the two combatants would fight until one or the other fell dead. It was not until Western-style competition was introduced into Japan that contests took on their present form.

Master Funakoshi used to say that "there are no contests in karate."

237–45. Old prearranged sparring

The meaning of the word itself has changed greatly, but even so, under present rules it is difficult to pick the winner. Perhaps the rules and the way contests are conducted will change in the future, and I think they should, but it is my opinion that "contests" cannot be held.

Although the exact date is not certain, it was during the early 1930s that prearranged sparring (*yakusoku kumite*) was created, developed, and came to be practiced in the dōjō. Free sparring (*jiyū kumite*) developed a few years later. (I do recall, however, that when I visited Okinawa in 1940, I saw no sparring; in fact, I heard that some karate-ka were ousted from their dōjō because they had adopted sparring after having learned it in Tokyo.)

There were three types of prearranged sparring. In the quintuple engagement match (*gohon kumite*), five consecutive punches were made against an opponent, the matter of whether they were to be upper level or middle level having been decided beforehand. When one got used to this, the wide dōjō seemed small, since the advancing and retreating movements became expansive.

The next to be performed was the triple engagement match (*sambon kumite*). In this the blocker would block and at the same time attempt to fill his opponent with the fear that the block would be painful. He also had to know how to block when the attacker delivered one punch after another. The attacker would consider ways of not having his punches blocked. He would practice throwing punches slowly or quickly, and he might try moving right into his opponent.

Sparring in this case might become virtually a melee, and it goes without saying that the man who had practiced longer or had a longer karate career would inevitably show the effects of his practice (and vice versa). In such a situation, it would be the one who was the rougher who would have the advantage. As a matter of fact, the striking and blocking techniques would be quite different from those of the kata. *Sambon kumite* properly practiced does not end in fighting, but there are those who practice in this way even now. It is strange that they do not realize that it is unnatural.

After the arms, legs and hips had been strengthened and the triple engagement match practiced thoroughly, the next type to be practiced was the single engagement match (*ippon kumite*). Here the stance was different, but it was decided beforehand who would be the attacker and who the blocker and whether the block would be upper level or middle level. While the attacker would try earnestly to find an opening, the blocker would try not to reveal an opening. Both took a low posture and made time, that is, waited for the other to show signs of tiring. The posture was itself tiring, but it was easier to spring forth and strike from a low position. On the other hand, the low posture made the target small.

It is easy to talk about an opening, but no one really knows what an opening is. Whatever the type of sparring, as two opponents become accustomed to each other, they will learn how to manage their power, and it will be difficult to find an opening, making it difficult to administer the decisive blow. To take an example, one man may plan to make his punch the decisive blow. The man who makes the decisive blow is the winner. But the loser, in trying to recover lost ground, may become excited. The performance may turn into a head-on battle, with both punching and blocking wildly without regard to fundamentals or kata. This is no longer prearranged sparring but free sparring—or to be more exact, a free-for-all fight.

If sparring is practiced by two of equal standing, the result will not be too serious, but in the case of a beginner against a senior, terrible things can happen. In this meeting of flesh with flesh, bone against bone, the pain can be extreme. It may be said to be a form of torture or a virtual baptism of pain. Still, in sparring, the fighting spirit is fostered.

To lessen the pain, one practiced assiduously on the striking post. He tried to increase the speed of his punch and also trained his arms by striking them repeatedly with some hard object. In other words, he subjected his body to all sorts of torture to lessen the pain of contact.

Today, we are practicing only one type of sparring, the prearranged single engagement match (*yakusoku ippon kumite*), because, with the change in the way of striking, it is no longer possible to practice the other prearranged sparring. So-called free sparring is also unnecessary now. The real meaning of sparring is in the contents of practice and can be understood naturally.

The present and former way of practicing sparring are the same in that a punch might be blocked in a number of ways, but with the present way of striking, a man can injure his opponent even if the blow does not land squarely. This is a fundamental difference, requiring effective defensive techniques. We were told to punch through our opponent, but actually we stopped our punches just before they made contact with the opponent's body, and the block had practically no power, for there is no need to practice defensive techniques if the way of striking is ineffectual. It was, so to speak, a matter of form, or going through the motions.

This should not be interpreted to mean that we did not practice with great earnestness. But I do think all the contradictions in the old way of training should be resolved, and effective striking and blocking should be studied thoroughly. If they are understood, then it is clear that sparring will change.

In practice, when your opponent throws a punch, you must be in motion when he punches. After you have seen your opponent move, is too late, and a false move on your part is out of the question, for your opponent's blow is pretty lethal. To move simultaneously with the punch, you must feel your opponent's intent.

One method of training to feel your opponent's intent, in either fundamentals or kata, is to practice under a command, learning to move with the command. When the command has ended, you must have finished your block. When the command is given, you must already be in motion. It is even better if you make the block simultaneously with the giving of the command. (The meaning of *simultaneously* must be stressed, i.e., at the exact instant, without a hairbreadth's difference in time.)

To do this, you must always keep cool, and your mind must be completely clear and as placid as that of a baby. But it is not a question of using your mind. You must move naturally without thinking about concentrating heart and soul in the technique. The time will come when you will concentrate them naturally without thought. When you reach this stage, you will succeed in moving simultaneously with the command.

Next, you should face your opponent with some distance between you, so that neither the punch nor the block can make contact. Let your opponent practice striking while you practice blocking. Repeat this until you can move simultaneously. Of course, you should change off and practice striking while your opponent practices blocking.

In a strict sense, this practice will not be practice in earnest, so you should next close the distance so that contact is possible. Practice in this way, but remember this is not a contest. This is practice. You cannot expect to make much progress if you are concerned about winning. Overconfidence will come from winning, and shame and the urge to act recklessly, from losing. You must not think about winning or losing, but if your opponent does succeed in striking you,

246–50. *Prearranged single engagement match*

study why the punch was effective. This is what practice is for. And since it is important to train hips and legs, practice over and over again.

At the next stage, let your opponent strike from the rear. This should not be done out of curiosity. Choose a time when there are few people around and your opponent from among your good friends. Obviously this type of practice will require even greater coolness than when you are facing your opponent, but it will contribute to the concentration of the mind.

If you think too much about the beginning of your opponent's strike, you will not be aware of his movements. Only when your mind is as placid as a still pond and you are physically very alert will you become aware of your opponent's movements and even his breathing in a natural way. (It might be mentioned that this is a potentiality not only of humans but of other animals.) In this state you will also naturally become aware of changes in your opponent's feelings. This is the meaning of being able to grasp, or feel, your opponent's intent.

If you stand behind your opponent and try to strike, he will naturally try to block, but you will come to know his reactions clearly. Do not think about what movements you will make. This is the most important thing. Be natural and move naturally. Do not try to go against nature. Your own body will become aware of your opponent's movements, even if you cannot see him.

After you have practiced with one opponent to the point that you can feel his movement with your own body, practice with three or five opponents.

With you standing in the center, let them throw punches without prior arrangement. Concentration of mind and body is of greatest importance, and your mind must be absolutely clear. There is no winner or loser, nor do you consider life or death. It is a state of nothingness. This may sound difficult, but it is not; only thinking makes it so.

Among the ancients, it was said that when one faces any opponent, he must be in a state of mind in which he is ready or able to die; that is, a state of mind in which life and death are irrelevant. In this state of mind, there will be no antagonism against the opponent, no winner and no loser, nor any feeling of fear or of hatred. You face your opponent with a clear mind. Thought is of no value; you simply act. Through practice one comes to understand this naturally.

"Keep your mind placid but be quick." I think these are appropriate words for a karate-ka. Your mind should be peaceful, but you should be ever on the alert to the happenings and movements around you. If not, you will not be able to cope if, for example, you are surrounded by several adversaries. A mind that is quiet and flexible, a body that is elastic and movements that are quick: these are the prerequisites of a karate-ka. To foster them, you must practice all the fundamentals and the kata. In mastering these, you will be able to achieve rhythm, timing, distance, breathing and the flow of vital energy.

In the seventeenth century, the Rinzai Zen priest-poet-calligrapher Bunan wrote a poem that says: "In the state of being dead while still living, one's actions are at their best." To understand this fully and translate it into practice is what I hope you will do.

The problem of mind is a very deep one. The elevation of the mind to a high state, the widening and purification of self, is the last thing to be achieved through practice. You must train mind and body, or practice has no meaning. Strive to cleanse the mind of the debris of everyday living. It is like washing potatoes in a tub of water; you should wash the dirt from your mind by coming into spiritual contact with others.

Mind and body are like the two wheels of a cart. Neither can be emphasized more strongly than the other. This is correct practice. To acquire what is valuable in life is true practice.

In coming into physical contact with others, you will come into spiritual contact. In daily life, you will come to know your relations with others, how everyone influences others and how ideas are exchanged. You should come to respect others and to think warmly of them. A budō-ka must be well-rounded and always bear in mind the happiness and welfare of others.

Words are easy to utter; putting them into action is not so easy. If you have an idea, put it into action immediately. This is what practice is for. If you cannot act, then your practice has been insufficient or you have some weak point.

Intend to get all you can from practice, but when you knock on the door of the dōjō, do not think about graduating. There is no such thing as graduating, at least as far as ordinary and plain men are concerned.

Kumite, I would like to say in conclusion, is the pursuit of karate as a fighting art to the very end—but eventually beyond that to the transcending of combat. Then you will be one with your opponent.

Appendix I

Practice from a Sitting Position

There is a type of practice done from a sitting position (*suwari geiko*), which used to be engaged in only for exhibition purposes and seems not to have been systematized. It existed not only in karate but in judo, *kendō*, *aikidō* and other martial arts. Although beginners were made to practice it at one time, it disappeared rather suddenly. Whether this was because it was considered useless or because it was too severe (that is, too much for the youth of today) is unclear. Perhaps practice from a standing position was thought to be more convenient as a starting point. But the contrary is true.

The first point with regard to this type of practice is that the hips and legs are greatly strengthened. Every movement must be based on the hips. In practice from a standing position, the hips may not be strengthened much. Thus, regardless of its severity, practice from a sitting position is necessary if the hips are to become strong and supple.

Moreover, even those who have practiced from a standing position for years should, I believe, practice from a sitting position in order to confirm whether they are actually using their hips in executing movements. The outcome may be that they are not even able to move when they try to practice in this way. Such people should start all over again.

The second point is the development of a body that is soft and flexible, without which one's movements cannot flow smoothly, and one cannot execute a technique fully.

This type of practice should always be done with a partner; otherwise, you will not be able to understand your own movements.

In karate, there are only a few types of sitting practice. They begin with the two opponents facing each other in the *seiza* position (figures 251 and 252).

One raises his knee and strikes. The blocker may block and retaliate with his own punch, as shown in figures 253 and 254.

Or the blocker may move quickly to the side to avoid the blow and then attack with a roundhouse or crescent-moon kick, as shown in figures 255 and 256.

He might also jump up and then kick. Of course, there are other

251. Seiza

252. Bow

253. Upper-level strike and block

254. Right punch counterattack

255. Middle-level attack

256. Roundhouse kick counterattack

257. *Upper-level kick and block*

258. *Retaliate by throwing*

259. *Upper-level strike and block-attack*

260. *Right straight punch*

261. *Iron hammer strike*

possibilities to be developed for application of various techniques, as shown in figures 257 through 261.

In this practice, one should prepare carefully and give due consideration to the meaning of the movements. I would recommend beginning with striking techniques.

There are also throwing techniques in karate. It is wrong to think they should not be practiced because striking or kicking are easier; with only striking and kicking techniques, karate remains only a fighting technique and in this way is unsatisfactory. Throwing techniques were practiced in my day, and I recommend that you reconsider them. I would advise consulting *Karate-dō Kyōhan: The Master Text* regarding them.

Appendix II

Yin and Yang

Aun, a word found in Yoga, Taoism, Buddhism and Shinto, is a term signifying heaven and earth, Yin and Yang—the cosmic dual forces: positive and negative, active and passive, male and female, the sun and the moon, and so on. All the universe is interpreted in terms of Yin and Yang and *aun*. *A* means heaven and is expressed in expiration (an open mouth), and *un* signifies earth and is expressed in inspiration (a closed mouth).

There is also the expression *aun gattai* (the union of Yin and Yang). It is said that everything has been created by *aun*, or Yin and Yang, and that heaven and earth, the positive and the negative, united to form the universe and all the creatures in it. Man, compared with the great universe, is the small universe.

One who practices karate should consider *aun* and Yin and Yang. He should, for example, consider the relationship between the hand that strikes and the hand that is withdrawn, between the hand that blocks and the hand that is withdrawn. It is to be hoped that he will come to have a good grasp of the relationships, of Yin becoming Yang and Yang becoming Yin.

Through the practice of the exercise known as *aun no gyō*, one seeks the root of the universe, of heaven and earth and of the human being.

To practice this exercise, you must be oblivious of your surroundings. You must forget yourself and cleanse your mind of all unhealthy thought.

Begin from the natural stance. Inhaling deeply clasp one hand in the other, bend your knees and crouch. This is the position of *un* (figure 262). When you exhale, do so completely, and stand on your toes, stretching your body to the maximum. Raise your hands high above your head, spreading the fingers and bending the wrists. At the same time, open your eyes wide and look straight up at the sky; open your mouth wide and say "Ahhh—." This is the position of *a* (figure 263).

There are those who are afraid to do this openly, but this is wrong. Forget yourself. Forget your surroundings. Find a suitable place to perform this exercise and you will find yourself united with the universe. This is indeed a beautiful state of mind.

262. Un

263. A   *264.* A (*side view*)

Index and Glossary

aikidō, 78, 119

body and mind, 9, 15, 23, 42, 53, 100, 103, 107, 117
breathing, 24, 45, 65, 74, 81, 100, 105, 118
budō: way of the warrior
Bunan, 118

changes, 9, 16, 41, 66, 76, 78, 81, 103
chōshi: rhythm
chūdan: middle or chest area
chūdan shutō-uke: middle-level sword-hand block
coexisting, 10, 15
combat, 13, 41, 49, 76, 80, 111
contest, 14, 111
cooperation, 14
counterattack, 84

defense, 79, 103
distance, 65, 77, 81, 105, 118
dō: the way

egotism, 10, 42, 78, 108, 122
elasticity, 66, 90

first strike, 19
flexibility, 23, 117, 119
front punch, 71, 74
fudō-dachi: immovable stance
Funakoshi, Gichin, 9, 11, 15, 18, 48, 58, 64, 74, 88, 111

Funakoshi, Gigō (Yoshitaka), 12, 48, 58, 75, 103
fundamentals, 41, 65

gedan: lower area of body
gedan-barai: lower-level block
gohon kumite: quintuple engagement match
gonen goroshi, 77
grappling, 79
gyaku hachiji-dachi: reverse natural stance

hachiji-dachi: natural stance
harmony, 18, 43, 66
heisoku-dachi: feet-together stance
hyōshi: timing

intent, 80, 115
ippon kumite: single engagement match

jiyū kumite: free sparring
jōdan: upper or face area
jōdan age-uke: upper-level rising block
judo, 78, 119
jutsu: technique

kakaekomi, 28, 54, 55
kamae: fixed posture
Kanō, Jigorō, 11
kata, 18, 41, 64, 96, 111
katachi: form or shape

keage: side-up kick
kebanashi: side-thrust kick
keiko: practice
keirei: salutation or bow
kekomi: side-thrust kick
kendō, 78, 119
ki: vital energy
kiba-dachi: horse-riding stance
kōkutsu-dachi: back stance
kokyū: breathing
kongō-mi, 51
kongō-shin, 51
kongō-riki, 51
kumite, 41, 65

life or death, 14, 117
low stance, 41

mae geri: front kick
makiwara: striking post
ma no torikata, 65, 77
mawashi geri: roundhouse kick
mayoko: sideways position
mental preparedness, 52
middle-level strike, 70
mikazuki-geri: crescent-moon kick
misconception, 10
moro-geri: simultaneous kick

nagewaza: throwing techniques
Nakayama, Hakudō, 11
natural movement, 9, 19, 80, 94, 98, 115, 119
natural stance, 43, 91, 98, 103
nature, 18, 116, 122
nekoashi-dachi: cat-leg stance
nidan: two levels
nidan-geri: double kick
ninjutsu, 12
nuki-ashi, 57

offense, 52, 79, 103
opening, 18, 113

power, 19, 55, 66, 78, 79, 80, 88, 90, 103, 115
practice, 15, 23, 78, 81
pseudo art, 14

real practice, 9, 20, 42
rei: ceremonial bow
reigi: etiquette, courtesy, politeness
relaxing, 24, 44, 66, 74, 80, 90, 106
renshū: training
reverse punch, 71, 74
rhythm, 52, 65, 77, 81, 105, 118
rigidity, 10, 43, 45, 46, 66, 75, 80, 105
Rō Sensei: old teacher

sambon kumite: triple engagement match
sanchin-dachi: hourglass stance
sandan-geri: triple kick
sankaku-tobi: triangular jump
sannen goroshi, 77
seiken, regular fist
seiza, 36, 119
shiko-dachi: square stance
Shimoda, Takeshi, 11, 75, 100
shizen-tai: natural position
shutō-uke: sword-hand block
sideways position, 88, 91
sokutō: outer edge of foot
sonoba gyaku-tsuki, 74
sōsoku-geri: simultaneous kick
soto uke: outside block
spirit, 13, 14, 44
striking post, 67, 68, 72, 111, 114
sumō, 46
suppleness, 10, 23, 42, 62, 99

suri-ashi, 46

teishō-barai: palm heel block
tettsui uchi: iron hammer strike
three essential points, 105
throwing techniques, 52, 121
timing, 52, 65, 77, 81, 105, 118
torite: throwing techniques
training, 15, 23, 78, 81
transcending combat, 42, 53
transcending life and death, 53, 118
tsuki: striking

uchi-uke: inside block
ude uke: forearm block
uke: blocking
unity, 15, 42
upper-level strike, 70

uraken: back fist

victory and defeat, 15, 42, 111
vital energy, 65, 85, 105, 118

Waka Sensei: young teacher
way, the, 9, 78
winning and losing, 14, 115

yakusoku ippon kumite: prearranged
  single engagement match
yakusoku kumite: prearranged sparring
Yin and Yang, 100, 107, 122
yōi: ready posture
yoko-geri: side kick

zenkutsu-dachi: front stance

Head Office and Branches of the Japan Karate-dō Shōtō-kai

Domestic Branches

Head Office & Shōtō-kan
Kashiwagi Building 2F, 1-4-2 Shibaura, Minato-ku, Tokyo 105-0023   03-3452-7983

Sub office
304 Dai-2 Ishigami Building, 1-15-6 Shibaura, Minato-ku, Tokyo 105-0023   Noriyuki Terui 03-3456-2969

Sapporo Branch
2-3-21 Ichijo, Kawazoe, Minami-ku, Sapporo-shi 005-0801   Kazuhiko Sekine   011-571-1727

Yamagata Branch
17-24 Shinmachi, Ienaka, Tsuruoka-shi, Yamagata 997-0000   Yoshitaka Hayashi 0235-23-6097

Tochigi Aikokai
2024 Iigai, Mooka-shi, Tochigi 321-4405 Hiromi Takamatsu   025-83-2729

Nihon Victor Karate Club Maebashi
1-10-1 Oowatari-machi, Maebashi-shi, Gunma 371-0854   Yoshiharu Tomaru   0272-51-4231

Higashi Iruma Dojo
665-9 Kamekubo, Ooimachi, Iruma-gun, Saitama 356-0051   Sigenobu Kuroiwa 0492-66-9229

Tateyama Branch
2426 Kamisanagura, Tateyama-shi, Chiba 294-0038   Fusando Sanada   04702-2-4557

Karate Senbukai

Senbukan Dojo
4-35 Yayoicho, Inage-ku, Chiba-shi, Chiba 263-0022   Hiroshi Takahashi   043-351-6622

Takane Branch
1-10-13 Shin Takane, Funabashi-shi, Chiba 274-0814 Kiyoshi Seki   0474-66-6743

Sakuragi Branch
489 Sakuragi, Wakaba-ku, Chiba-shi, Chiba 264-0022   Yoshio Toyota   043-231-2373

Shirako Branch
2526-5 Shirako-machi, Chosei-gun, Chiba 299-4200   Tadayuki Kono   0453-3-3548

Kawado Branch
142-5 Kawado-machi, Chuo-ku, Chiba-shi, Chiba 260-0802   Minoru Sakata   043-264-0364

Takasu Branch
3-2-8-105 Takasu, Mihama-ku, Chiba-shi, Chiba 261-0004   Toshio Matsuda   043-279-0499

Noro Branch
623-50 Noro-machi, Wakaba-ku, Chiba-shi, Chiba 265-0053   Hisao Takekawa   043-228-3907

Anesaki Branch
8 Daijuku, Sodegaura-shi, Chiba 299-0241 Shigeo Shirahama   0438-63-3641

Ichikawa Branch
6-22-12 Soya, Ichikawa-shi, Chiba 272-0832 Hiroshi Kudo   0473-71-5883

Seifukan Karate Dojo
26-32 Matsukaze-machi, Hiratsuka-shi, Kanagawa 254-0812   Hitoshi Kobayashi   0463-21-2396

Victor Company of Japan Karate Club
3-12 Moriya-machi, Kanagawa-ku, Yokohama-shi, Kanagawa 221-0022   Tsutomu Higuchi 045-783-7259

Nihon Victor Co MP Business Dep QC Sec.
1612-1 Kami Tsuruma, Yamato-shi, Kanagawa 242-0004   Takao Yamaji   0462-75-1111

Senshu University Physical Training Association Karate Club
2-1-1 Higashi Mita, Tama-ku, Kawasaki-shi, Kanagawa 214-0033   044-911-7131

318 Kanda, Jinbo-cho, Chiyoda-ku, Tokyo 101-0051   03-3265-6211

Ninomiya-cho Karate-do Association
217 Ninomiya, Ninomiya-cho, Naka-gun, Kanagawa 259-0123   Hajime Akiyama 0463-23-2933

Chuo University Schoolmate Association Karate Club
742-1 Higashi Nakano, Hachioji-shi, Tokyo 192-0351   Dojo 0426-74-3887

Chuo University Schoolmate Physical Association
Nanpei Ryo, 7-7-8 Minamihira, Hino-shi, Tokyo 191-0041   0425-92-4265

Gakushuin University Karate-do Club
1-51 Mejiro, Toshima-ku, Tokyo 171-0031
03-3996-0221

Seijo University Physical Association Karate-do Club
6-1-20 Seijo, Setagaya-ku, Tokyo 157-0066
03-3484-6078

Tokyo-Tocho Karate-do Club
2-8-1 Nishi Shinjuku, Shinjuku-ku, Tokyo 160-0023   Sumio Shibata   03-3770-4120

Tokyu Karate Dojo
4-11-14 Minami Yukigaya, Oota-ku, Tokyo 145-0066   Kiyoshi Akutsu   03-3729-5730

Taisei Corporation Karate-do Club
Shinjuku Center Building, 1-25-1 Nishi Shinjuku, Shinjuku-ku, Tokyo 163-0690   Nobuaki Tanaka
03-3348-1111

Mitsui & Co., Ltd. Karate-do Club
1-2-1 Otemachi, Chiyoda-ku, Tokyo 100-0004
Seishiro Itakura   03-3285-1111

Sakura Bank Karate-do Club
1-3-1 Kudan Minami, Chiyoda-ku, Tokyo 102-0074   Hidemitsu Nakao   03-3230-3111

Tokyo Noko University Doshi Association
1-15-6-2-304 Shibaura, Minato-ku, Tokyo 105-0023   Nobu Maemura   03-3456-2969

Mudo Juku
3-31-14-803 Miharadai, Nerima-ku, Tokyo 177-0031   Ken Nakamura   03-3923-7564

Mitsubishi Real Estate Karate Club
Tokyo Building, 2-7-3 Marunouchi, Chiyoda-ku, Tokyo 100-0005   Masataka Kozono
03-3287-5167

Niigata Dokokai
318 Kamitakada, Sasakami-mura, Kitakanbara-gun, Niigata 959-1973   Toshihiko Igarashi
02506-2-6008

Nagoya Doyukai
1-13-203 Monzen-cho, Naka-ku, Nagoya-shi, Aichi 460-0018   Hisaichi Ozeki
052-321-9453

Osaka Kubotakai
1-2-4 Fushimidai, Inagawa-cho, Kawabe-gun, Hyogo 666-0262   Kenichi Nonaka
0727-66-1422

9-12 Minamigaoka, Kawachi Nagano-shi, Osaka 586-0065   Tsutomu Shimizu   0721-62-5268

Hiroshima Branch
2-9-10 Ishiijo, Fuchu-cho, Aki-gun, Hiroshima 735-0007   Hiroshi Ishihara   0822-84-2278

Kishodo Building, 9-34 Hondori, Naka-ku, Hiroshima-shi, Hiroshima 730-0035 Shin Kumano
082-248-0901

Kudamatsu Branch
1638 Higashitoyoi, Kudamatsu-shi, Yamaguchi 744-0002   Fumio Makiyama   0833-41-3925

Kochi Branch
206-14 Yokohama, Kochi-shi, Kochi 781-0240
Tadao Tanida   0888-41-0279

Tosa Yamada Branch
1505-28 Kusume, Tosa Yamada-cho, Kami-gun, Kochi 782-0051   Hitoshi Tokuhiro
08875-3-5161

Kagoshima Branch
2-12 Yamashita-cho, Kagoshima-shi, Kagoshima, 892-0816   Shunji Nakamura   0992-22-2188

Foreign Branches

Taiwan Branch
158-12 Shintoku Hokuji, Taichu-shi, Taiwan Province, China   Teinan Rin

Spain Shoto-kai
Pza. Dr. Laguna o 9.3 oE, Madrid 28009, Spain
Atsuo Hiruma   279-6489

France Shoto-kai
Tour des Herizons 67, rue Pierre Brossolette 92320 Châtillon, France   Pierre Preneron

Portugal Shoto-kai
R. Horetense Luz-5, 2825 Vila De Caparica, Portugal   Mario Rebola

K.D.S
22 Shakespeare Road, St. Dials Cwmbran, Gwent, nP44 4LW Great Britain   Michisuke
Harada   633-862803

Italy Shoto-kai
Via Carducci, 12-47044 Igea, Marina, Italy
Alp Roberto